JN014362

オンラインで受けられる
CNN英語検定
公式ガイド

笹尾洋介 監修

京都大学 国際高等教育院
附属国際学術言語教育センター 准教授

朝日出版社

音声ダウンロードの方法

本書の音声データは、下記の方法でご利用いただけます。

音声ファイル（MP3）ダウンロード

MP3形式の音声ファイルを下記のURLよりダウンロードし、iTunesやWindows Media PlayerなどのMP3再生が可能なソフトに取り込んで聴くことができます。
ダウンロードしたファイルをパソコン上でiTunesやWindows Media Playerなどに取り込んだ上で、ポータブルオーディオ機器やスマートフォンなどに同期してご利用いただくこともできます。

 https://www.asahipress.com/cet/20kentei/mp3.zip

アプリ「リスニング・トレーナー」で音声ダウンロード

アプリ「リスニング・トレーナー」を使って音声をスマートフォンやタブレットにダウンロードし、聴くことできます。

●「リスニング・トレーナー」の使い方

① App StoreまたはGoogle Playから「リスニング・トレーナー」のアプリ（無料）をダウンロード。

 App Storeはこちら   Google Playはこちら

② アプリを開き、「コンテンツを追加」をタップ
③ 画面上部に【01189】を入力しDoneをタップ

※ スマートフォンなどの端末をお使いの場合、
　音声ファイルやアプリをダウンロードする際には、Wi-Fi環境での接続を推奨いたします。
　また、3G・LTE回線での通信時は、パケット通信料定額サービスのご利用を推奨いたします。

Contents

TEST 1

TEST 2

解答・解説

「CNN英語検定」について

☞「CNN英語検定」とは

▶「CNN英語検定」は、20億人が視聴する世界最大のニュース専門テレビ局CNNのニュースをテスト問題に使用し、英語のリスニング能力とリーディング能力を測定するものです。

英語学習誌『CNN ENGLISH EXPRESS』誌に、2018年6月号以来5回にわたり掲載された「CNN英語検定」をもとに、オンラインテストとして開発が進められ、2020年3月6日からプレテストが受験できるようになりました。'20年7月6日からは第2回プレテストが公開されています。

☞「CNN英語検定」の特長

▶「CNN英語検定」の最大の特長はCNNの生きたニュースをテスト素材として使い、グローバルなニュースを理解する「時事英語力」を測るテストであるということです。

従来の英語能力テストのリスニング音声は、大半がスタジオ録音のクリアな発音です。日常生活で話される英語に比べてはるかにクリアな上、実際にはしばしば起こる音声変化が含まれていません。そのためテストでは聞けても、実際の会話やテレビ・映画の英語は聞き取れないという事態が起こりがちです。

これに対し、CNNニュースの英語は、日常生活のさまざまな場面で使われている生きた英語であり、世界各国の英語のさまざまなアクセントを含みます。実際の場で聞き取る必要がある多様な英語が、リスニング能力の判定に使われています。

▶ リーディングセクションの素材も、リスニングセクションと同様にCNNのニュースであり、話題性のある新しい情報を扱っています。そのため、一般的な英語力に加えて、ニュース英語に特徴的な表現や近年話題になっている政治・経済・文化などに関する知識も必要となります。

▶ 配点はリスニングセクションが60点、リーディングセクションが40点となっています。リスニングの配点が大きいことが「CNN英語検定」の大きな特長の1つです。

☞ オンライン受験

▶ コンピューターやスマホ、タブレットなどの携帯端末とインターネット接続があれば、24時間いつでも、受けたいときに好きな場所で受けられます。

▶ 自動採点なので、試験終了後、結果がすぐに表示されます。

☞ 申し込み方法

以下のURLから、オンラインで24時間申し込みができます。

https://www.asahipress.com/special/eigo_kentei/

☞ 問題構成

「CNN英語検定」の問題構成は以下の通りです。

	配点	問題数	試験時間
リスニングセクション	60点	30	約27分
リーディングセクション	40点	20	25分

合計 ▶ 50問／100点満点／約52分　　　　　　　　　　　　※試験時間はそれぞれ目安です。

CNNとは

CNN（Cable News Network）は、最新ニュースを24時間配信し続ける国際放送ネットワーク。本社のあるアメリカはもとより、世界200以上の国と地域で、20億人以上が視聴している。

傾向と対策 | リスニングセクション

リスニングセクションはPart 1〜 Part 4からなり、試験時間は約27分※です。

▶ 問題に関する指示文・指示音声はすべて英語です。

▶ 問題文の音声は、Part 1とPart 2では2回、Part 3とPart 4では1回流れます。

▶ Part 1のディクテーション問題では空所に該当する単語をタイピング入力します。他のPartは三肢択一式問題です。

▶ リスニングセクションで問われる設問は、以下の4種類です。

	設問構成	設問内容	設問数
1	**書き取り**	ディクテーション	4
2	**大意把握**	ニュースの主題を問う	7
3	**詳細理解**	ニュースの中で重要な細部を問う	15
4	**話者の意図推測**	話者の発言の意図を推測する	4

合計 ▶ 30問／配点60点

▶ 配点の大きいリスニングセクション（60点）にうまく対応することがスコアを上げる大きなポイントになりますが、リスニングの練習でスタジオ録音のクリアな音声ばかり聴いていた場合、CNNのナチュラルスピードの音声が聞き取れないことが多いかもしれません。

　これは、ネイティブスピーカーが話す場合、特に単語の語尾の音にしばしば変化が起こり、そのために聞き取りにくいことが1つの原因です。そこで生の英語に対応するためには、こうした音声変化を知っていることが大切です。代表的な音声変化については、p.13の解説をご覧ください。

※リスニングセクションの試験時間はテストごとに多少変わります。

Part 1　ディクテーション問題

▶ 問題は2題出題されます。

▶ 20〜30秒程度のニュース（またはニュースの一部）を聴き、英文の空所に聞き取った単語を入力します。音声は2度流れ、2度目の音声の後に30秒間、タイプする時間がありますから、焦る必要はありません。空所は1題につき2箇所あります。

▶ 入力する単語は1語のみです。単語の前後にスペースが入っていたり、語頭が大文字になっていたりすると誤りになりますから、注意が必要です。

例題1

Thought-controlled ①_____ arms may sound like a thing of the future, but they have become reality. Scientists at Johns Hopkins University created the ②_____ limbs.

訳 思考制御型ロボットアームと聞くと、未来のもののように思えるかもしれませんが、現実のものとなっています。ジョンズ・ホプキンス大学の科学者たちがこの義肢を開発しました。

正解 ① robotic   ② artificial

例題2

Well, the World Health Organization is calling for a crackdown on ①_____ cigarettes. It wants governments to ②_____ people smoking them indoors.

訳 世界保健機関（WHO）は、電子たばこの取り締まりを勧告しています。WHOは、各国政府に屋内での電子たばこの喫煙を禁止するよう求めているのです。

正解 ① electronic   ② ban

Part 2　ショートニュース問題

► 問題は3題出題されます。
► 30〜40秒程度の短めのニュースを聴き、1題につき2問の設問に答えます。
► 設問は選択肢3つの中から答えを選ぶ三肢択一式です。
► ニュースの音声が2回流れた後に設問の音声も流れ、そのあと解答時間が15秒あります。

例題3

Researchers have found the world's oceans are soaking up much more heat than we understood before. The oceans take in 90 percent of the excess heat trapped in Earth's atmosphere. The levels of oxygen and carbon dioxide in the air increase as the oceans warm and release gases. The study estimates oceans have absorbed 60 percent more heat than previously thought. All of this could result in faster-rising sea levels, more powerful storms and more melting of sea ice.

訳　研究者たちによると、世界の海が、従来の理解よりもはるかに多くの熱を吸収しています。海は地球の大気中にこもった余剰熱の90％を吸収しています。海水温度が上昇し、海からガスが放出されるにつれ、空気中の酸素と二酸化炭素の量も増えます。この研究の推計によれば、海は従来考えられていたよりも60％多くの熱を吸収しているということです。これらの現象は、海面の上昇を加速させたり、より勢力の強い暴風雨やいま以上の海氷の融解をもたらしたりする可能性があります。

▶ 設問の内容は「大意把握」が1問、「詳細理解」が1問になります。

設問例

[**大意把握**]

● **What is the main point of the news report?**

　　訳　このニュースの主旨は何ですか。

● **What is the news report mainly about?**

　　訳　このニュースは主に何について述べていますか。

● **What problem in the US is the main topic of the news report?**

　　訳　米国のどのような問題がこのニュースの主題ですか。

● **What is the main problem that the researcher in the news report has to solve?**

　　訳　このニュースに出てくる研究者が解決しなければならない主な問題は何ですか。

[**詳細理解**]

● **What have researchers discovered about the oceans?**

　　訳　研究者たちが海について発見したこととは何ですか。

● **What was unusual about this beauty contest?**

　　訳　この美人コンテストで珍しかったことは何ですか。

● **What does this gene do?**

　　訳　この遺伝子はどのような働きをしますか。

● **Why are companies like Google offering more paid leave?**

　　訳　グーグルなどの企業がより多くの有給休暇を与えようとしているのはなぜですか。

Part 3　ニュース問題

▶ 問題は2題出題されます。

▶ 2分前後の長めのニュースを聴き、5問の設問に答えます。設問は選択肢3つの中から答えを選ぶ三肢択一式です。

▶ ニュースの音声が1回流れた後に設問の音声も流れ、そのあと解答時間が15秒あります。

▶ 設問の内容は「大意把握」が1問、「詳細理解」が3問、「話者の意図推測」が1問になります。

設問例

[話者の意図推測]

● **What does Musk imply about his plan to build a city on Mars?**

　　訳　マスク氏は、火星に都市を建設するという彼の計画についてどのようなことを示唆していますか。

● **What does Obama think about the spread of COVID-19?**

　　訳　オバマ氏は新型コロナウイルス感染症の拡大についてどのように考えていますか。

「大意把握」と「詳細理解」の設問例はp.8の「ショートニュース問題」の解説を参照してください。

例題略

Part 4　インタビュー問題

▶ 問題は2題出題されます。

▶ 3分～3分30秒程度のインタビューを聴き、5問の設問に答えます。設問は選択肢3つの中から答えを選ぶ三肢択一式です。

▶ インタビューの音声が1回流れた後に設問の音声も流れ、そのあと解答時間が15秒あります。

▶ 設問の内容は「大意把握」が1問、「詳細理解」が3問、「話者の意図推測」が1問になります。

「大意把握」と「詳細理解」の設問例はp.8の「ショートニュース問題」の解説、「話者の意図推測」は上記の解説を参照してください。

例題略

傾向と対策 | リーディングセクション

リスニングセクションの解答制限時間がきたら、「This is the end of the Listening Section. Please go on to the Reading Section now.」とアナウンスが流れますので、**画面下の「Reading Sectionへ進む」をクリック／タップして、リーディング問題に進みます。**

► Part 1〜Part 3からなり、試験時間は25分です。

► リーディングセクションは、「前へ」ボタンで、前の問題に戻ることができるので、わからない問題は飛ばして先に進み、あとで戻って解答することができます。

► リーディングセクションで問われる設問は、以下の4種類です。

	設問構成	設問内容	設問数
1	**語彙**	ニュースの理解に必要な語彙力を問う	4
2	**大意把握**	ニュースの主題を問う	5
3	**詳細理解**	ニュースの中で重要な細部を問う	9
4	**話者の意図推測**	Part 3の長文問題で、話者の発言の意図を推測する	2

合計 ► 20問／配点40点

Part 1　語彙問題

► 問題は4題出題されます。

► ニュースから抜粋した英文に空所が設けられており、そこに入る最も適切な単語を3つの選択肢の中から選びます。

例題1

In less than 50 years, the working population could (　　　　) by nearly half. Already, firms complain of labor shortages, and the ratio of job openings to applicants has reached a 40-year high.

(**A**) leapfrog　　　(**B**) blossom　　　(**C**) shrink

訳 50年もしないうちに、労働人口が半数近くに減るかもしれません。すでに、企業は労働力不足を嘆いており、有効求人倍率はこの40年で最高に達しています。

正解 **C**

例題2

Exercise is one of the factors proven to have a big impact on our (　　　). It reduces the risk of heart disease, the number-one killer in the United States.

(**A**) duration 　　　(**B**) longevity 　　　(**C**) offspring

訳 運動は、寿命に大きな影響を及ぼすことが証明されている要因の1つです。アメリカで最も多い死因である心臓疾患のリスクを減らしてくれるのです。

正解 **B**

Part 2　短文読解問題

▶ 問題は3題出題されます。

▶ 150語程度の短めのニュースを読み、各2問の設問に答えます。選択肢3つの中から答えを選ぶ三肢択一式です。

例題3

Navigating the streets of New Delhi is proving difficult right now. Thick smog currently blankets the city, prompting the Indian Medical Association to declare a public-health emergency.

"Schools should be closed down. People should not step out of their homes, especially the elderly, pregnant ladies, children, and heart and asthma patients." (Dr. Krishan Kumar Aggarwal, Former President, Indian Medical Association)

City officials say the air-quality index, which measures the concentration of harmful substances in the air, reached a dangerously high level of 451 this week out of a maximum of 500. Anything over 100 is considered unsafe.

> Forecasters say there is no relief in sight for at least the next few days.
>
> For now, Delhi's schools remain closed, and if the heavy pollution persists or worsens, city officials are discussing ways to reduce traffic on the capital's streets.

訳 ニューデリーの街を移動するのは今や難しくなっています。濃いスモッグが目下、市内を覆っており、インド医師会が公衆衛生上の非常事態を宣言するに至っているのです。

「学校は休校にすべきです。住民は外出を避けるべきです、特にお年寄り、妊婦、子ども、心臓疾患やぜんそくの患者は」(クリシャン・クマール・アガーワル医師　インド医師会前会長)

市当局によると、空気中の有害物質の濃度を示す大気質指数が今週、最高値500のところ、451という危険な高レベルに達したということです。100を超えると危険な数値とされます。

気象予報士は、少なくともあと数日間は、状況は良くならないと言います。

現在、デリー市内の学校は休校となったままで、深刻な汚染が続くか悪化する場合に備えて、市当局は首都市街の交通量を緩和する方法を議論しています。(**138 words**)

▶ 設問の内容は「大意把握」が1問、「詳細理解」が1問になります。「大意把握」と「詳細理解」の設問例はリスニングセクションのp. 8の「ショートニュース問題」の解説を参照してください。

Part 3　長文読解問題

▶ 問題は2題出題されます。

▶ 500語程度の長めのニュースを読み、各5問の設問に答えます。選択肢3つの中から答えを選ぶ三肢択一式です。

▶ 設問の内容は「大意把握」が1問、「詳細理解」が3問、「話者の意図推測」が1問になります。「大意把握」「詳細理解」の設問例はリスニングセクションのp. 8の「ショートニュース問題」の解説を、「話者の意図推測」の設問例はリスニングセクションのp. 9の「ニュース問題」の解説を参照してください。

例題略

ナチュラルスピードの英語の 音声変化 に慣れよう

CNNニュースをはじめ、ネイティブスピーカーが話すナチュラルスピードの英語では、単語の語尾の音にしばしば変化が起こり、そのことがリスニングを難しくしている原因の1つとなっています。こうした英語を聞き取るには、音声変化の現象を知っておくことが必要です。そこで、代表的な音声変化である「連結」「脱落」(または「同化」)「破裂が聞こえない破裂音」について説明します。

💬 連結 linking

「連結」は、前の単語の語尾の子音と、次の単語の語頭の母音または子音がつながって、1つのまとまった音として発音される現象です。この現象は、ナチュラルスピードだけでなく、ゆっくり話される英語でも起こります。

[例] ① My coat got dirty when I leaned against the wall.
（壁にもたれたときにコートが汚れてしまった）

② Let's take a rest under that tree.
（あの木の下で一休みしよう）

💬 同化 assimilation

連続した音をスムーズに発音しようとして、前の音または後ろの音の一方が、あるいは2つの音が1つに混じり合って、別の音に変化する現象を「同化 (assimilation)」と言います。たとえば、[t] や [d] の音のあとに [j] 音が続くと、[tʃ] や [dʒ] の音に変化することがあります。

[例] ① I can't wait for next year's FIFA World Cup.
（来年のFIFAワールドカップが待ち遠しい）

② Don't call me unless you really need to.
（本当に必要なとき以外は電話しないで）

💬 脱落 deletion

子音が連続すると発音しにくいため、2つの子音に挟まれた [t] や [d] の音は、脱落すること
があります。また、同じ音の子音や似たような音の子音が連続する場合にも、脱落が起こるこ
とがあります。

［例］　① I pass**(ed)** my driving test on my firs**(t)** try.
（運転免許試験に1回で合格した）

　　　② This ferry is design**(ed)** to carry up to 500 passengers.
（このフェリーの旅客定員は500人だ）

💬 破裂が聞こえない破裂音 no-audible-release plosives

破裂音（[p] [t] [k] [b] [d] [g]）は、すぐ後ろに別の子音（特に破裂音・鼻音）が続く場合、
破裂が聞こえないことがあります。

　また、[t] の音は、すぐ前に母音（または [l] [r] [n]）があり、すぐ後ろに別の子音が続く場
合、口の中で [t] の音を発音する構えさえつくらないことがあり、代わりに、息を止めたような
間が聞こえます（これは、[t] の音の後ろに何も続かない場合や、母音が続く場合でも起こる
ことがあります）。

［例］　① Don'**t** le**t** this opportunity sli**p** by.
（このチャンスを逃さないようにね）

　　　② I find i**t** har**d** to ma**ke** time for exercise.
（運動のために時間をつくるのは、私には難しい）

TEST 1

Listening Section

Part 1

Directions

Here are the directions for **Part 1**. You will hear two short news reports. Enter the missing words in the spaces below the text. Enter only one word in each blank space. You will hear each report two times. For each report, after listening two times, you will have 30 seconds to enter the missing words.

No.1

The influential European Investment Bank says it will end ①(   ) for fossil-fuel projects by 2022 as part of a new energy-lending policy to tackle climate change. This is a pretty big deal. The new focus will be on clean-energy innovation, the policy unlocking €1 trillion for ②(   ) investment.

Enter the word for ①

Enter the word for ②

No.2

Astronauts on the International Space Station are getting a sweet delivery. Now, they'll be able to actually bake cookies. NASA is sending up a new space oven on this cargo flight that ①(   ) Saturday from Virginia. The resupply capsule is set to dock with the station later on Monday. The toaster oven will test how baking works in low ②(   ).

Enter the word for ①

Enter the word for ②

Part 2

Directions

Here are the directions for **Part 2**. You will hear three short news reports. Each report will be followed by two questions. You will hear each report two times and each question only once. For each question, you will have 15 seconds to choose the best answer.

問題文 設問

| No.1 | |

1. **What is the main point of the news report?**

   (**A**) NASA discovered a planet where life might be possible.

   (**B**) NASA found three new dwarf stars outside our solar system.

   (**C**) A new planet was found in our solar system.

2. **According to the news report, what can help to warm a planet?**

   (**A**) Water on its surface

   (**B**) An atmosphere dense enough to trap heat

   (**C**) Being within 31 light years of a star

問題文 設問

| No.2 | |

1. **What is the main point of the news report?**

   (**A**) About 11 billion tons of ice were sent to Greenland to replace melted ice.

   (**B**) Melted ice will be used to keep people cool during heat waves.

   (**C**) Greenland's ice sheet has been melting very quickly.

2. **What is a result of warmer temperatures around the world?**

   (**A**) Ocean levels are rising.

   (**B**) Millions of swimming pools have been closed.

   (**C**) Ice sheets are expanding.

問題文　設問

No.3

1. What is the main lesson that the couple should have learned?

(**A**) Keeping money is always better than spending it.

(**B**) You should never pay for an SUV with cash.

(**C**) You should not spend money that is not yours.

2. What was the couple probably going to have to do?

(**A**) Make payments only by credit card

(**B**) Repay more than $100,000

(**C**) Tell their bank about the mistake

Part 3

Directions

Here are the directions for **Part 3**. You will hear two news reports. Each report will be followed by five questions. You will hear each report and question only once. For each question, you will have 15 seconds to choose the best answer.

問題文　設問

No.1

1. **What is the main problem that the women in the news report face?**

   (**A**) There is too much competition for a small number of jobs.

   (**B**) They are expected to have a large number of children.

   (**C**) They must work under harsh conditions without proper maternity care.

2. **What does the news report say about the tea industry in Assam?**

   (**A**) Its workers enjoy India's highest standards of healthcare.

   (**B**) Not all its plantations offer adequate medical care to workers.

   (**C**) It exports tea through government agencies.

3. **What does the news report say about tea plantations in Assam?**

   (**A**) They pay workers by the hour.

   (**B**) They don't employ pregnant women.

   (**C**) Most of their workers are women.

4. **What does the reported comment by the health director imply?**

   (**A**) That Assam's maternal death rate will continue to rise

   (**B**) That the state government already has a plan to improve the situation

   (**C**) That nothing more can be done about the problem

5. **What is reported about female tea pickers in Assam?**

   (**A**) Some give birth in the fields where they work.

   (**B**) They usually quit their jobs as soon as they become pregnant.

   (**C**) They get a full day's pay when they take a day off to give birth.

問題文 設問

No.2

1. **What is the news report mainly about?**

   (**A**) Growing concern about e-cigarettes

   (**B**) The need for more funding to fight an epidemic

   (**C**) The policy of Juul Labs

2. **What caused many people to worry?**

   (**A**) A large donation by the Bloomberg charity

   (**B**) A surge in e-cigarette advertising

   (**C**) A sudden increase in cases of lung illness

3. **What was Juul Labs warned about?**

   (**A**) Giving people the wrong impression about its products

   (**B**) Putting additives into its e-cigarettes

   (**C**) Targeting nicotine users

4. **What does the governor of New York probably think about e-cigarettes?**

   (**A**) That a ban on all smoking will solve the problem

   (**B**) That more information about their safety is needed

   (**C**) That the problem is not as serious as the media has reported

5. **What caused the reported illnesses and deaths?**

   (**A**) Misleading advertising

   (**B**) An additive

   (**C**) The cause is still unclear.

Part 4

Directions

Here are the directions for **Part 4**. You will hear two interviews. Each interview will be followed by five questions. You will hear the interviews and each question only once. For each question, you will have 15 seconds to choose the best answer.

問題文　設問

No.1

1. What is the interview mainly about?

(**A**) Sanitation in slum areas

(**B**) Progress toward meeting global challenges

(**C**) Solutions to the problem of climate change

2. Why is it hard to introduce modern sewer systems into developing countries?

(**A**) Because people in those countries are not used to them

(**B**) Because the cost is too high for such countries

(**C**) Because such countries have very large populations

3. How is human waste treated in the newly developed toilets?

(**A**) It is burned.

(**B**) It is flushed away in clean water.

(**C**) It is buried in ash.

4. What is a major problem with the newly developed toilets?

(**A**) They are not suitable for tourist areas.

(**B**) They are still too expensive.

(**C**) They cannot treat a large enough volume of waste.

5. What does Gates seem to think about the world's big problems?

(**A**) Nuclear war and pandemics are the biggest of them all.

(**B**) They will cause a rise in childhood death.

(**C**) We may solve them if the trend of progress continues.

Listening Section

No.2

1. What are the main opinions expressed by Cameron in this interview?

(**A**) The UK and the US disagree too much, and the Iran deal had to be replaced.

(**B**) UK-US teamwork is crucial, and the US should have stayed in the Iran deal.

(**C**) The UK-US relationship is traditional, and the Iran deal caused instability.

2. On what topic did Cameron say he agrees with Trump?

(**A**) Free trade

(**B**) Climate change

(**C**) Fighting terrorism

3. What did Cameron say was the basic benefit of the Iran deal?

(**A**) It would make sure that Iran did not get nuclear weapons.

(**B**) It would keep Iran from supporting Islamist extremists.

(**C**) It would allow Iran to join NATO.

4. What did Cameron imply about the Iran deal he helped to negotiate?

(**A**) That it had too many imperfections

(**B**) That it could work only while Obama was president

(**C**) That it guaranteed at least some degree of certainty

5. What view did Cameron say he shared with members of Congress?

(**A**) That Iran supports terrorist groups

(**B**) That Iran promotes stability in the Middle East

(**C**) That the West shouldn't expect Iran to be perfect

Reading Section

Part 1

Directions

Part 1 contains four short excerpts from news reports. Each excerpt has one blank space and is followed by three answer options. Choose the best word from the answer options to fill each blank space.

No.1

Two minke whales became the first (　　　　) on the day Japan officially resumed commercial whaling for the first time in 30 years.

(**A**) casualties　　　(**B**) detriments　　　(**C**) offerings

No.2

Jewels belonging to Marie Antoinette have (　　　　) a queen's ransom at auction.

(**A**) accorded　　　(**B**) fetched　　　(**C**) sought

No.3

More than 70 years after the Holocaust, there are a/an (　　　　) few survivors to pass on their memories.

(**A**) abating　　　(**B**) dispersing　　　(**C**) dwindling

No.4

The president turned his (　　　　) on climate commitments in the name of jobs and economic growth.

(**A**) back　　　(**B**) head　　　(**C**) palm

Part 2

Directions

Part 2 contains three short news reports, each followed by two questions. For each question, choose the best answer from the answer options.

No.1

Rethinking Workplace Robots

Robots are an increasingly common part of the manufacturing workforce. In Germany, for example, Volkswagen uses robots to manufacture cars. Robots seem to be competing with humans for jobs, and the World Economic Forum estimates that millions of jobs will be lost to robots in the next few years.

However, at German manufacturer SEW Eurodrive, robots are there to cooperate with humans, not replace them. These coworking robots ("cobots") do heavy manual labor, deliver parts and can spot mistakes that humans overlook. SEW says using robots allows the company to be more productive and expand its operations, which means it can hire more human workers.

1. **What is the main point of the news report?**
   (**A**) That robots cannot spot mistakes as well as humans can
   (**B**) That not all workforce robots take humans' jobs
   (**C**) That robots make more mistakes than humans do

2. **According to SEW, what has using robots enabled the company to do?**
   (**A**) Replace most of its workers with robots
   (**B**) Give its human workers some much-needed time off
   (**C**) Create more jobs for people

No.2

A Special Place Now Lost

A secret library in Syria was once a place of comfort and refuge where local residents, especially children, escaped the horrors of war around them and found solace among books. The chief librarian was a 14-year-old boy named Amjad, who was in charge of everything and spent many hours there.

The library was in Darayya, a suburb of Damascus, which was besieged by Syrian-government forces for nearly four years while rebels were in control of the area. The rebels made a deal with the government in August 2016, agreeing to hand over control of Darayya in exchange for safe passage out of the area. After the handover, Syrian-government soldiers took control of the town, and all the civilians were relocated to other areas. By then, Darayya had been completely destroyed, and the library was only a memory in the minds of Amjad and the other former residents.

1. **What is the news report mainly about?**
   (**A**) A welcome refuge amid war
   (**B**) A place where rebels held secret meetings
   (**C**) A change in the control of Darayya

2. **Who was in control of Darayya from August 2016?**
   (**A**) Rebel soldiers
   (**B**) A 14-year-old boy
   (**C**) The Syrian government

No.3

Delicate Dilemma for Mexico

Mexico has many migrants, most from Central America, traveling through the country in caravans with the goal of entering the United States. But their rising number, as well as changes in policy about them, have led to a humanitarian crisis.

The Mexican government had previously promised a more humane approach to the migrants and started granting temporary visas to some of them. But then it realized that it could not sustain the growing migrant population and reduced the number of visas it granted, leaving many people undocumented. Meanwhile, the United States has made it harder for the migrants to cross the US border, leaving many stuck in Mexico without visas or jobs.

The United States is also putting pressure on Mexico to limit migration into Mexico from the south. Mexico plans to boost economic development in its southern areas and in Central America as a way to reduce the number of migrants moving through the country.

1. **What is the news report mainly about?**
    (**A**) A humanitarian crisis in Mexico
    (**B**) Mexico's policy toward the United States
    (**C**) Economic development in Central America

2. **Why have many of the migrants been unable to reach their goal?**
    (**A**) Because they have run out of money and must stay and work in Mexico
    (**B**) Because it has become more difficult to enter the United States
    (**C**) Because they have become separated from the caravans

Part 3

Directions

Part 3 contains two news reports, each followed by five questions. For each question, choose the best answer from the answer options.

No.1

Starting a Revolution in Food

You may one day be able to eat burgers grown in space. Aleph Farms, an Israeli food company that engineers beef steaks from cow cells, has successfully grown meat on the International Space Station for the first time. This is a significant step toward the company's goal of commercially producing slaughter-free, ecofriendly meat.

Here's how it works. Researchers take cells from a cow, give them nutrients and put them in an artificial environment mimicking the inside of a cow's body. The cells then multiply, grow into connective muscle tissue and eventually become a full-sized steak. Aleph Farms collaborated with a Russian bioprinting company, 3D Bioprinting Solutions, to successfully carry out the process.

According to Aleph Farms, this cutting-edge research, conducted in some of the most extreme environments imaginable, indicates the growth potential of sustainable food-production methods that avoid the land waste, water waste and pollution that conventional beef production involves.

The space-grown meat could help feed astronauts during long-term manned space missions as well as address food insecurity among the booming population down on Earth, according to a statement by 3D Bioprinting Solutions. Aleph Farms says its products are not yet commercially available but will likely be ready for the market in three or four years.

Didier Toubia, CEO of Aleph Farms, told CNN that the factory-farming industry had "lost the connection with the animal" and that growing slaughter-free steaks was a better alternative to using cows "as mere machines to produce steaks."

The company says that the cell-based process is not only more humane but also better for the environment, one of its aims being to make meat with a minimal environmental footprint. Conventional beef production uses up a lot of land and resources. Cows grow and reproduce more slowly than pigs and poultry, so they eat a lot more and need more land and water. Beef alone is responsible for 41 percent of livestock greenhouse-gas emissions, and livestock accounts for 14.5 percent of total global emissions, according to the United Nations. That's more than direct emissions from the transportation sector.

"In space, we don't have 10,000 or 15,000 liters of water available to produce 1 kilogram of beef," said Toubia. "This joint experiment marks a significant first step toward achieving our vision to ensure food security for generations to come while preserving our natural resources."

These efforts come as the global climate crisis and population boom continue to grow. A World Resources Institute report in July 2019 found that Americans will need to cut their average consumption of beef by about 40 percent, and Europeans by 22 percent, for the world to continue to feed the 10 billion people expected to live on this planet in 2050. In the time until then, the global demand for meat and dairy is expected to rise by nearly 70 percent. The global demand for beef, goat meat and lamb or mutton is expected to rise even more, by 88 percent.

In the face of these looming environmental dangers coupled with rising food demands, many companies are trying to find solutions. Aleph Farms has competition: Mosa Meat in the Netherlands and Memphis Meats in the US are also racing to develop in vitro or "clean" meat. Plant-based protein brands like Impossible Foods and Beyond Meat have also exploded onto the food scene in recent years. Their meatless burgers have spread to Burger King, McDonald's, Tim Hortons and even grocery stores across the US.

1. **What is the main topic of the news report?**

   (**A**) The birth of a cow at the International Space Station

   (**B**) The environmental footprint of the traditional meat industry

   (**C**) Technology to grow meat outside of animals

2. **What is needed to begin growing steaks by the method Aleph Farms uses?**

   (**A**) Cells from a cow

   (**B**) Connective muscle tissue

   (**C**) An artificial environment for cows

3. **What does the news say is one of the merits of the new meat technology?**

   (**A**) It could improve global food security.

   (**B**) It would create many new jobs.

   (**C**) It would allow more cows to be used for milk instead of meat.

4. **What does the Aleph Farms CEO imply about conventional meat farming?**

   (**A**) Its products taste better than cell-based meat.

   (**B**) It is inhumane.

   (**C**) It produces more nutritious meat.

5. **How could switching to engineered steaks help the environment?**

   (**A**) More land could be used for raising pigs and poultry.

   (**B**) It would reduce transportation-sector emissions.

   (**C**) Fewer cows would mean lower greenhouse-gas emissions.

No.2

A Closer Look at Pigs

Pigs are not heralded for their intelligence, but swine are smarter than they seem. They are test subjects in studies that lead to lifesaving discoveries. They are reliable and beloved therapy animals. And now, we can add tool use to the list of their accomplishments.

According to a study in the journal *Mammalian Biology*, researchers observed a family of critically endangered Visayan warty pigs using sticks to dig and build nests— evidence that the digitless swine are capable of using tools. Pigs are not known for nest-building, and they certainly are not known for any sophisticated use of tools. They had never been observed using any before, a fact attributed to their lack of digits and their cloddish snouts. Meredith Root-Bernstein, a conservation ecologist and a coauthor of the study, stumbled across the phenomenon at a Parisian zoo, where she witnessed an adult warty pig named Priscilla digging with a stick in her mouth.

"She would deposit some leaves, move them to a different spot on the mound and dig a bit with her nose," Root-Bernstein wrote in her observations. "At one point, she picked up a flat piece of bark about 10 centimeters by 40 centimeters that was lying on the mound. Holding it in her mouth, she used it to dig—lifting and pushing the soil backward—quite energetically and rapidly."

Root-Bernstein was so captivated by Priscilla that she visited the enclosure again several times, in 2015, 2016 and 2017, with a team of researchers who placed spatulas in the pigs' area. The researchers wanted to see if and how Priscilla and her penmates would use the objects as tools. However, the pigs did little with the gadgets during the researchers' first visit. Then, in 2016, Priscilla and her female offspring moved sticks in a rowing motion to dig and build a nest. Priscilla's mate Billie also dug with a stick, though his attempts were not as successful as those of his female family members, the researchers wrote.

In the 2017 trial, Priscilla dominated once again, using a stick to dig a total of seven times. But the study noted that digging with sticks in their mouths was less effective than digging with their hooves or snouts. So why, then, did the pigs do it?

Perhaps they just enjoyed it. The researchers said the pigs might view tool use as a reward that "feels good." At least, it does not appear to harm their nest-building. Or perhaps the behavior is truly beneficial to nest-building and humans have yet to figure out why. The study could not determine just why the pigs kept digging.

In any case, the behavior was likely learned among Priscilla's family. Visayan warty pigs live in family units and, like human children, study each other to learn what goes right, according to the study.

Few species have been spotted using tools to their benefit, Root-Bernstein told CNN. Primates like chimpanzees and orangutans use tools to search for food. But pigs getting handy? It was virtually unheard of in science before her observation.

"Just using tools at all is very significant," she said. "At the time, there were no scientific reports on tool use in any kind of pigs."

According to Root-Bernstein, besides being a win for pigs in the intellectual-capacity department, the findings provide clues to how cognition evolves and how bodies are linked to their environments. "We might think that only humans manipulate the environment to affect their own lives," she said, "but in different ways, many other species do this too."

---

1. What is the news report mainly about?
(A) The fact that female pigs are smarter than male pigs
(B) A study about what pigs do for enjoyment
(C) The discovery that pigs use tools

2. **What was Priscilla seen doing with sticks?**

   (**A**) Digging

   (**B**) Looking for food

   (**C**) Moving mounds around

3. **Why did the researchers place spatulas in the pigs' enclosure?**

   (**A**) To make the pigs' nests more comfortable

   (**B**) To see if the pigs used them as tools

   (**C**) Because the pigs couldn't move things for themselves

4. **Which of the following would Root-Bernstein probably agree with?**

   (**A**) Cognition evolves only after the development of tool use.

   (**B**) Tool use is not a very significant development.

   (**C**) Our usual ideas about animal intelligence need changing.

5. **What did Root-Bernstein say her research can help us understand?**

   (**A**) How to manipulate the environment better

   (**B**) How cognition develops

   (**C**) What kind of species pigs evolved from

TEST 2

Listening Section

Part 1

Directions   28↓

Here are the directions for **Part 1**. You will hear two short news reports. Enter the missing words in the spaces below the text. Enter only one word in each blank space. You will hear each report two times. For each report, after listening two times, you will have 30 seconds to enter the missing words.

No.1   29↓

Well, there's optimism about two new ①(   ) for Ebola. They're proving so effective they're being offered to all patients in the Democratic Republic of Congo, where the current ②(   ) is the second-deadliest ever. Eighteen hundred people have died since last summer.

Enter the word for ①

Enter the word for ②

No.2   30↓

New figures released Wednesday by the Institute of International Finance show combined US public- and private-sector ①(   ) was close to $70 trillion. In just simple terms of dollars and cents, America's national ①(   ) hits a new record high every second, ②(   ) $23 trillion right now, about $68,000 for every man, woman and child.

Enter the word for ①

Enter the word for ②

Part 2

Directions

Here are the directions for **Part 2**. You will hear three short news reports. Each report will be followed by two questions. You will hear each report two times and each question only once. For each question, you will have 15 seconds to choose the best answer.

問題文　設問

No.1

1. **What is the main point of the news report?**

   (**A**) Humans have altered the land to make it more suitable for animals.

   (**B**) Humans are to blame for a number of environmental problems.

   (**C**) Humans are responsible for the recent decrease in ocean pollution.

2. **What does the news report say has happened since 1980?**

   (**A**) Ocean plastic pollution has increased 10 times.

   (**B**) Around 1 million species of animals have become extinct.

   (**C**) Around 75 percent of all land has been altered.

問題文　設問

No.2

1. **What is the news report mainly about?**

   (**A**) Global banking

   (**B**) Improvements in education

   (**C**) Gender equality

2. **Which country was found to be the least gender-equal?**

   (**A**) The Democratic Republic of the Congo

   (**B**) Saudi Arabia

   (**C**) The United States

問題文 設問

No.3

1. What is the main point of the news report?

(**A**) The measles virus is no longer a threat in developed countries.

(**B**) The incidence of measles is on the rise around the world.

(**C**) The measles virus has been eliminated in the US.

2. What happened in the US in the year 2000?

(**A**) The number of measles cases skyrocketed.

(**B**) There were three times more measles cases than in 2018.

(**C**) Measles was declared to have been eliminated.

Part 3

Directions

Here are the directions for **Part 3**. You will hear two news reports. Each report will be followed by five questions. You will hear each report and question only once. For each question, you will have 15 seconds to choose the best answer.

問題文　設問

No.1

1. **What is the main issue discussed in the news report?**
   (**A**) A GoFundMe page for a California teacher
   (**B**) Increasing cases of cancer among public-school teachers
   (**C**) Sick-leave policy for California teachers

2. **What did the sick teacher have to pay for?**
   (**A**) 100 days of sick leave
   (**B**) Disability insurance under a state program
   (**C**) A substitute to teach her classes

3. **What is true about public-school teachers in California?**
   (**A**) They must pay for substitutes to teach their classes if they take extended leave.
   (**B**) Teachers with serious illnesses are not allowed to take extended sick leave.
   (**C**) Disability insurance pays their salaries when they are on sick leave.

4. **What can be inferred from the statement by the San Francisco teachers union?**
   (**A**) The union is asking schools to hire more substitute teachers.
   (**B**) The union will address the sick-leave problem through contract negotiations.
   (**C**) The number of sick days that teachers can take cannot be increased.

5. **What have some educators said is to blame for the situation in California?**
   (**A**) The increasing number of teachers with serious illnesses
   (**B**) A lack of funding for public education
   (**C**) The rising cost of hiring substitute teachers

Listening Section

No.2

1. What problem in the UK is the main topic of the news report?

(**A**) Children having to deliver food to earn money

(**B**) Worsening lack of food among the poor

(**C**) Breaches of policy by human-rights campaigners

2. What criticism has been made of the UK government?

(**A**) That it has not made sure that citizens have enough food

(**B**) That it has prevented charities from helping hungry families

(**C**) That its policies have forced many food banks to close

3. Who has been supplying food aid to needy citizens in the UK?

(**A**) Charities

(**B**) Campaigners

(**C**) Policymakers

4. What did the report by Human Rights Watch say about single mothers?

(**A**) They deliver food parcels to make money.

(**B**) They send their children to food banks to ask for food.

(**C**) They sometimes miss meals in order to feed their children.

5. What does the statement by the government spokesperson imply?

(**A**) The government has sent needy children to live in wealthy households.

(**B**) The government is giving working families money to relocate.

(**C**) The criticism against the government does not reflect reality.

Part 4

Directions

Here are the directions for **Part 4**. You will hear two interviews. Each interview will be followed by five questions. You will hear the interviews and each question only once. For each question, you will have 15 seconds to choose the best answer.

問題文　設問

No.1

1. **What aspect of Jane Goodall's life is the interview mainly about?**

    (**A**) Her travels in Africa

    (**B**) Her research on chimpanzees

    (**C**) Her family relationships

2. **What did Goodall learn from her mother that she passes on to others?**

    (**A**) You should try to bring opportunities to deprived communities.

    (**B**) Even boring jobs can be opportunities.

    (**C**) You should work very hard and never give up.

3. **What led to the extension of funding for Goodall's research?**

    (**A**) Her visit to the National Geographic Society

    (**B**) Her discovery of a chimpanzee that used tools

    (**C**) Her discovery of a rare, white ape

4. **What does Goodall imply about dealing with chimpanzees?**

    (**A**) Showing them how to use tools increases their trust.

    (**B**) If they don't come to trust you quickly, they never will.

    (**C**) Variety and change make them cautious.

5. **According to Goodall, how do chimpanzees reassure each other?**

    (**A**) By making physical contact

    (**B**) By sitting down and waiting

    (**C**) By giving each other palm-oil nuts

Listening Section

No.2

1. What is the interview mainly about?

(**A**) Privacy in social media

(**B**) Concerns about Facebook

(**C**) The history of antitrust laws

2. What view did the interviewer present about Facebook and the free market?

(**A**) Because Facebook is free, it has no responsibility to users.

(**B**) Facebook should pay users for the data they provide.

(**C**) Users agree to give up their privacy when they use Facebook.

3. What did Hughes mean when he said that Facebook is not really free?

(**A**) Facebook cannot be considered a free service because it is a monopoly.

(**B**) It costs a lot of money to run a company like Facebook.

(**C**) Users give Facebook their data in exchange for using the service.

4. What is the accountability problem that Hughes mentioned?

(**A**) Mark Zuckerberg does not really have to answer to anyone.

(**B**) Facebook's board of directors has too much power over Zuckerberg.

(**C**) Facebook is subject to regulation by the FTC.

5. What did Hughes say about corporate governance?

(**A**) Making a profit should be the only goal of corporate governance.

(**B**) Corporations should fulfill a broad range of social responsibilities.

(**C**) Corporate boards do not have environmental responsibilities.

Reading Section

Part 1

Directions

Part 1 contains four short excerpts from news reports. Each excerpt has one blank space and is followed by three answer options. Choose the best word from the answer options to fill each blank space.

No.1

The wind turbine was designed specifically to (   ) power, and today almost 4 percent of the world's electricity is produced by wind.

(**A**) generate   (**B**) project   (**C**) regulate

No.2

In 2016, the Chinese government changed the (   ) one-child policy. Each couple is now allowed to have two babies.

(**A**) expensive   (**B**) notorious   (**C**) predictable

No.3

Huge numbers of Cambodian migrants are fleeing Thailand. They are worried about a possible crackdown on (   ) workers.

(**A**) undocumented   (**B**) discredited   (**C**) unrecognizable

No.4

The Trump administration hopes to make military (   ) into the final frontier, the depths of outer space.

(**A**) objections   (**B**) interventions   (**C**) inroads

Part 2

No.1

The Growing Threat of Superbugs

According to a new report, drug-resistant infections are expected to dramatically increase across the globe. The main culprit is the overuse of antibiotics, which are not the solution we tend to think they are. Superbugs that cause drug-resistant forms of diseases are growing fast and may claim more lives than cancer by the year 2050.

The study also talks about economic impact. It predicts that related global costs will spiral upwards to $100 trillion or more, a figure larger than the current annual world GDP of $70 trillion.

The world's poorest nations are most at risk. Nine million of the estimated 10 million deaths will be in Africa and Asia. The aim of the study is to sound the alarm and call for global action.

1. **What is the news report mainly about?**
   (**A**) Lifestyle diseases
   (**B**) Drug-resistant infections
   (**C**) Drug overdoses

2. **What kind of economic impact is expected?**
   (**A**) Costs will be very high around the world.
   (**B**) The annual world GDP will increase.
   (**C**) No impact is expected in Africa and Asia.

No.2

Chocolate for a Better World

A Dutch company is determined to fight slavery, and their weapon of choice is chocolate. More than 2 million people work in the cocoa industry under such illegal practices as trafficking and child labor, and Tony's Chocolonely wants to help fix that.

Tony's buys cocoa beans only from ethical farm cooperatives in West Africa. The beans are ground into liquid chocolate, which is then molded by Belgian chocolate masters. Each chocolate bar is stamped with unequal shapes to reflect inequality in the world, a reminder to chocolate consumers of why Tony's Chocolonely began.

However, labor abuses in cocoa production remain in the headlines. According to a 2015 study, more than 2 million child laborers are exposed to hazardous conditions. Endemic poverty was cited as a major reason why trafficking and unethical practices continue. Tony's believes their business model can improve the situation. They want to set an example for bigger companies toward solving the problem of slavery in the value chain of cocoa.

1. **What is the news report mainly about?**
   (**A**) Efforts to end slavery in the cocoa industry
   (**B**) A new marketing approach for chocolate
   (**C**) Ways to send ethical messages to consumers

2. **According to the 2015 study, why do the unethical practices continue?**
   (**A**) Because of trafficking
   (**B**) Because of hazardous conditions
   (**C**) Because of poverty

No.3

Sniffing Out Dangers

Dogs have a sense of smell that is infinitely better than ours. However, an extraordinary sensor is now helping humans to sniff the air for anything dangerous, including diseases.

The sensor is a microchip that detects chemicals in the air, and it works like a tiny digital nose. It uses the unique fingerprint of a chemical to identify it among all the molecules present in the air.

The sensor can be used in different ways. It can detect different sorts of smells and can also tell how much of something is present. It can detect down to levels of parts per billion. That's equivalent to one drop in an Olympic-size swimming pool.

The microchip was developed by combining expertise in chemistry, electronics and nanotechnology. It is already tiny, but work continues to shrink it further for the healthcare market. The plan is to use the microchip in mobile phones to detect compounds on the breath that indicate illnesses like cancer, tuberculosis and asthma.

1. **What is the main point of the news report?**

   (**A**) A new smell sensor has been developed.

   (**B**) A new device is being used to detect diseases in dogs.

   (**C**) Technology is helping people who have lost their sense of smell.

2. **Where will the new device be used after it is made even smaller?**

   (**A**) In the pet industry

   (**B**) In the healthcare market

   (**C**) In fingerprinting

Part 3

No.1

Nigeria's Little-Known Space Program

When you think about space exploration, Cape Canaveral and the International Space Station probably come to mind. Here is another place to add to that list: Nigeria. That's right, Nigeria has a space program, implemented by the National Space Research and Development Agency (NASRDA).

"We're not part of the race for the moon. We're not part of the race for Mars. The space program in Nigeria has always been focused on bringing practical solutions to Nigeria's problems," says Seidu Onailo Mohammed, NASRDA's director general.

It might seem surprising that Nigeria, a country with spotty electricity, a 70 percent poverty rate and a life expectancy of 53 years, would fund a space program. Even Nigerians who work there have had a hard time believing it. Sadiya Bindir, an engineer at NASRDA says, "I was initially surprised that Nigeria had a space agency, and now when I tell my friends where I work, they're all, like, 'Oh, we have such an agency?'"

But researchers here say satellite images are key to understanding big problems like rapid urbanization, a swelling population and a looming food crisis. The space agency is also using its satellites to look for almost 300 schoolgirls kidnapped in 2014 by Boko Haram.

The agency has eight locations, including the Centre for Satellite Technology Development (CSTD) in the capital city, Abuja. Its sprawling campus is home to a ground station, a conference center and even a museum. The laboratories look more like high school science classrooms. But the agency has put five satellites in orbit since

2003. However, those satellites were not built or launched on Nigerian soil.

So far, Nigeria's space program has outsourced its heavy lifting. For example, Russia and China have launched Nigeria's previous Earth-observation and communication satellites. Handling such operations within Nigeria itself is the next goal. CSTD's Abubakar Sadiq Umar, an engineer who worked on those designs, says it is a matter of national pride: "We should be able to take what we've seen abroad and transplant it here in Nigeria so that we can have our own satellite that we'll be proud of."

Perhaps the most ambitious goal is to put the first African astronaut into space by 2030. "Putting a man in space," says Umar, "is one thing everybody tends to appreciate, and is a goal that every country wishes to actualize. And my country, Nigeria, cannot be left out."

Nigeria has allocated about $20 million to the space agency for the current year. But why should the government be spending so much money during these tough economic times? Director General Mohammed says more money is always needed: "This is the same question that has always been asked in the US. 'Why waste money on NASA?' But a budget for satellites is also a budget for agriculture, and it's also a budget for the environment. Is money for the space agency a waste? To me, it is not."

1. **What is the main topic of the news report?**

   (**A**) The purpose of Nigeria's space program

   (**B**) Efforts to improve Nigeria's electricity supply

   (**C**) Nigeria's plan to put the first African astronaut on the moon

2. **What does the news report say about Nigeria's space program?**

   (**A**) It boosts the country's economy by creating new jobs.

   (**B**) It is not well known.

   (**C**) Its laboratories have cutting-edge technology.

3. **According to the news report, for what purpose has Nigeria used satellite images?**

   (**A**) To find solutions to some of the country's social problems

   (**B**) To improve its electricity supply

   (**C**) To look for habitable places on Mars

4. **What is a new goal that Nigeria hopes to achieve in the future?**

   (**A**) To open a museum to exhibit the country's achievements in space

   (**B**) To build a satellite in Nigeria

   (**C**) To use satellite images to understand shifts in population

5. **What does Mohammed probably think about NASA?**

   (**A**) Its achievements are worth the money spent on it.

   (**B**) Too much money has been wasted on it.

   (**C**) It should focus more on agriculture and the environment.

No.2

National Service for National Unity

The American economy is on solid footing. Now in its 120th month of expansion, it shows few signs of bubbles about to burst. Unemployment is way down, inflation is contained, and wages are finally moving up. And perhaps most significantly, productivity is up. There is no denying that economic indicators are firmly positive.

These good numbers, however, are unlikely to change another set of numbers, regarding the geography of growth. Mark Muro of the Brookings Institution has calculated that over the last decade, the 53 largest American metro areas have accounted for 71 percent of America's total population growth, two-thirds of all of its employment growth, and a staggering three-quarters of all of its economic growth. In fact, half of all job growth in the United States took place in just 20 cities. Meanwhile, small towns in rural America have lost residents and barely contributed anything to economic growth.

This two-track economy has produced a two-track culture, with urbanites and rural Americans increasingly living in their own distinct worlds of news, entertainment and consumer goods. They live different lives and disagree deeply about politics—a trend that is reflected in Washington.

Why is this happening? The economic trends can be explained by the digital revolution and globalization, in which brain work is more valuable, brawn work less so. The cultural forces are related to the recent rise of identity politics and backlash against immigration and multiculturalism. We see the forces that are pulling America apart. The question we should be focused on is, what can we do to bring the country together? Surely this has become the question of our times.

One answer that I have been increasingly drawn to is national service. There are many ways to design a national-service program, and a voluntary system will probably work better if it has strong incentives, like loan forgiveness and tuition support, at its core. A 2013 study argued that current programs could feasibly be scaled up to 1 million volunteers without taking jobs from existing workers and would yield societal benefits worth more than four times the cost of the programs. And the programs that are already in operation, such as AmeriCorps, do good work and have stunningly high approval ratings from their alumni. Ninety-four percent say they gained a better understanding of differing communities, and 80 percent say the program helped their careers.

As Mickey Kaus noted in a prescient 1992 book, John F. Kennedy, the wealthy graduate of Choate and Harvard, famously served in World War II on a PT boat alongside men who held jobs like mechanic, factory worker, truck driver and fisherman. Imagine if in today's America, the sons and daughters of hedge-fund managers, tech millionaires and bankers spent a year with the children of coal miners and farmers, working in public schools or national parks or the armed forces.

National service will not solve all of America's problems, but it might just help bring us together as a nation, and that is the crucial first step forward.

1. **What is the main problem that the report identifies?**

   (**A**) America has become deeply divided.

   (**B**) Immigration issues are America's biggest concern.

   (**C**) America is facing a slowing economy.

2. **What did Mark Muro conclude about the United States?**

   (**A**) That most of its recent economic growth has happened in cities

   (**B**) That its small towns have been expanding rapidly

   (**C**) That its urban areas and rural areas have been developing at an even pace

3. What does the reporter mean by "two-track culture" in the third paragraph?

(**A**) Identity politics versus multiculturalism

(**B**) Immigrants versus Americans

(**C**) Rural culture versus urban culture

4. Why is John F. Kennedy mentioned in the news report?

(**A**) Because Kennedy wrote a book on national service

(**B**) To illustrate the point about wealthy youth working for the national good

(**C**) Because Kennedy started a program like the one the reporter recommends

5. What does the reporter say about national service?

(**A**) It could take away many existing jobs.

(**B**) It is too much of a sacrifice for young Americans.

(**C**) It might be a way to bring Americans together again.

解答・解説

TEST 1

解答欄にご自身の解答を書き写しておくと、スコアを出しやすくなります。

Listening Section リスニング編

Part	No.	Question	解答欄	正解	測定する力
1	1	1		financing	書き取り
		2		sustainable	書き取り
	2	1		launched	書き取り
		2		gravity	書き取り
2	1	1		A	大意把握
		2		B	詳細理解
	2	1		C	大意把握
		2		A	詳細理解
	3	1		C	大意把握
		2		B	詳細理解
3	1	1		C	大意把握
		2		B	詳細理解
		3		C	詳細理解
		4		B	話者の意図推測
		5		A	詳細理解
	2	1		A	大意把握
		2		C	詳細理解
		3		A	詳細理解
		4		B	話者の意図推測
		5		C	詳細理解
4	1	1		B	大意把握
		2		B	詳細理解
		3		A	詳細理解
		4		B	詳細理解
		5		C	話者の意図推測
	2	1		B	大意把握
		2		C	詳細理解
		3		A	詳細理解
		4		C	話者の意図推測
		5		A	詳細理解

Reading Section リーディング編

Part	No.	Question	解答欄	正解	測定する力
1	1	——		**A**	語彙
	2	——		**B**	語彙
	3	——		**C**	語彙
	4	——		**A**	語彙
2	1	1		**B**	大意把握
		2		**C**	詳細理解
	2	1		**A**	大意把握
		2		**C**	詳細理解
	3	1		**A**	大意把握
		2		**B**	詳細理解
3	1	1		**C**	大意把握
		2		**A**	詳細理解
		3		**A**	詳細理解
		4		**B**	話者の意図推測
		5		**C**	詳細理解
	2	1		**C**	大意把握
		2		**A**	詳細理解
		3		**B**	詳細理解
		4		**C**	話者の意図推測
		5		**B**	詳細理解

スコア （配点は各2点です）	リスニング（30問） ／60	リーディング（20問） ／40	合計 ／100

上の表から、それぞれの「測定する力」の正解数を数え、下の欄に記入しましょう。
あなたの強みと弱点が一目でわかります。

リスニング	書き取り ／4	大意把握 ／7	詳細理解 ／15	話者の意図推測 ／4
リーディング	語彙 ／4	大意把握 ／5	詳細理解 ／9	話者の意図推測 ／2

TEST 1

Listening Section リスニング編

Part 1 ディクテーション問題

No.1

オーストラリア英語

The influential European Investment Bank says it will end ①<u>financing</u> for fossil-fuel projects by 2022 as part of a new energy-lending policy to tackle climate change. This is a pretty big deal. The new focus will be on clean-energy innovation, the policy unlocking €1 trillion for ②<u>sustainable</u> investment.

訳

影響力の大きい欧州投資銀行は、2022年までに化石燃料事業への融資を終了すると発表しました。気候変動対策に向けたエネルギー関連融資に関する新方針の一環としてです。これはかなり大きな出来事です。新たな融資対象は革新的なクリーンエネルギー技術となり、新方針によって、1兆ユーロが持続可能な（エネルギーへの）投資に充てられるようになります。

語句

influential: 影響力のある／financing: 融資／fossil-fuel: 化石燃料の／tackle: （問題などに）取り組む／climate change: 気候変動／big deal: 大きな出来事／innovation: 革新／unlock: ～を利用できるようにする／trillion: 1兆／sustainable: 持続可能な ▶ここではsustainable-energy の意。／investment: 投資

No.2

南アフリカ英語

Astronauts on the International Space Station are getting a sweet delivery. Now, they'll be able to actually bake cookies. NASA is sending up a new space oven on this cargo flight that ①<u>launched</u> Saturday from Virginia. The resupply capsule is set to dock with the station later on Monday. The toaster oven will test how baking works in low ②<u>gravity</u>.

訳

国際宇宙ステーションの宇宙飛行士たちは、素晴らしい配送物を受け取ることになっています。これで、なんと飛行士たちはクッキーを焼くことができるようになります。NASA（米航空宇宙局）が、土曜日にバージニア州から飛び立ったこの貨物専用機で宇宙空間用の新しいオーブンを配送中なのです。補給カプセルが月曜日に宇宙ステーションとドッキングする予定です。オーブントースターは、低重力での焼き具合をテストされることになっています。

語句

astronaut: 宇宙飛行士／sweet: 素晴らしい、好ましい ▶「甘い」の意味をかけている。／delivery: 配送物／bake: ～を（オーブンなどで）焼く／cargo flight: 貨物専用機の便／launch: 〈ロケットなどが〉打ち上がる／resupply: 補給／be set to do: ～することになっている／dock with: ～とドッキングする／later: ▶「何時になるかわからないが、月曜日（放送時）のこの後」ということ。／work: 〈事が〉運ぶ／low gravity: 低重力

Part 2 ショートニュース問題

<table>
<tr><td>No.1</td><td>問題文 ⑫↓ 設問 ⑬↓
アメリカ英語</td></tr>
</table>

1. 正解 A

What is the main point of the news report?

(A) NASA discovered a planet where life might be possible.
(B) NASA found three new dwarf stars outside our solar system.
(C) A new planet was found in our solar system.

設問訳 このニュースの主旨は何か。

(A) NASA が、生命が存在する可能性のある惑星を発見した。
(B) NASA が、われわれの太陽系外に3つの新しい矮星を見つけた。
(C) われわれの太陽系で新しい惑星が1つ見つかった。

解説 冒頭で NASA has discovered a nearby super-Earth that just might support life.（NASA が、生命を維持する可能性を秘めた［地球から］近距離のスーパーアースを発見した）と述べられており、これを言い換えた（A）が正解となる。（B）は「その米国の宇宙機関（＝ NASA）が31光年ほどの位置にある矮星を周回する惑星を3つ発見した」の部分を変えて「3つの矮星を発見した」とした錯乱肢。NASA は「太陽系外で」惑星を探していたところ、新たな惑星を見つけたので、（C）も不正解。

2. 正解 B

According to the news report, what can help to warm a planet?

(A) Water on its surface
(B) An atmosphere dense enough to trap heat
(C) Being within 31 light years of a star

設問訳 このニュースによると、惑星を温めるのを助けうるのは何か。

(A) 惑星表面の水
(B) 熱を閉じ込めるのに十分に濃い大気
(C) ある星から31光年以内にあること

解説 最後に if its atmosphere is dense enough, it could trap heat to warm the planet（もしその大気が十分に濃いものであれば、惑星を温める熱を閉じ込めて

おける）と述べられている。it could trap... の it は前述の「十分に濃い大気」を指している。つまり、惑星を温めるには熱を閉じ込める必要があり、熱を閉じ込めるためには大気が濃いものでなければならないので、正解は（B）。

問題文　An Interesting Discovery in Space

NASA has discovered a nearby super-Earth that just might support life. The US space agency was looking for planets outside of our solar system, and it found three of them orbiting a dwarf star just about 31 light years away. Wow. Researchers say one planet is within the star's habitable zone. Scientists believe if its atmosphere is dense enough, it could trap heat to warm the planet and also allow for water and life on the surface.

訳　宇宙における興味深い発見

NASA が、生命を維持する可能性を秘めた（地球から）近距離のスーパーアースを発見しました。その米国の宇宙機関がわれわれの太陽系外の惑星を探していたところ、31光年ほどの位置にある矮星（わいせい）を周回する惑星を3つ発見したのです。驚きです。研究者たちによれば、そのうちの1つの惑星は、その矮星の生命居住可能領域内にあるということです。科学者たちの考えでは、もしその大気が十分に濃いものであれば、惑星を温める熱を閉じ込めておける上、その地表に水や生命が存在するのを可能にするとのことです。

語句

super-Earth: スーパーアース、巨大地球型惑星 ➤地球の数倍から10倍程度の質量を持ち、地球に比較的近い成分でできた太陽系外惑星のこと。／ the US space agency: ➤NASA を指す。／ solar system: 太陽系／ orbit: ～を周回する／ dwarf star: 矮星（わいせい）／ just about: だいたい、およそ／ light year: 光年／ planet: 惑星／ habitable zone: ハビタブルゾーン、生命居住可能領域／ atmosphere: 大気／ dense:〈密度が〉濃い／ trap: ～を閉じ込める／ allow for: ～を可能にする／ surface: 表面

No.2

問題文 ⑭↓ 設問 ⑮↓

アメリカ英語

1. 正解 C

What is the main point of the news report?

(**A**) About 11 billion tons of ice were sent to Greenland to replace melted ice.

(**B**) Melted ice will be used to keep people cool during heat waves.

(**C**) Greenland's ice sheet has been melting very quickly.

設問訳 このニュースの主旨は何か。

(**A**) 解けた氷の代替として約110億トンの氷がグリーンランドに送られた。

(**B**) 熱波の間、人々の体を涼しく保つために解けた氷が使われることになる。

(**C**) グリーンランドの氷床が急速に解けている。

解説 冒頭の Climate change is causing the ice to melt in Greenland in alarming amounts.（気候変動によって、グリーンランドで憂慮すべき量の氷が融解している）や、続く Greenland's ice sheet experienced its biggest melt of the summer（グリーンランドの氷床ではこの夏最大の融解が生じ）…losing 11 billion tons of surface ice to the ocean（表面の110億トンの氷が［解けて］海に流れ出た）などと述べられていることから、このニュースが（**C**）の「氷床の融解」について伝えていることがわかる。

2. 正解 A

What is a result of warmer temperatures around the world?

(**A**) Ocean levels are rising.

(**B**) Millions of swimming pools have been closed.

(**C**) Ice sheets are expanding.

設問訳 世界各地の気温上昇がもたらしたこととは何か。

(**A**) 海面水位が上昇している。

(**B**) 何百万もの水泳プールが閉鎖している。

(**C**) 氷床が拡大している。

解説 気候変動がもたらしたこととして、このニュースで真っ先に述べられているのが「氷の融解」である。（**C**）の「氷床が拡大している」はこれと正反対なので不適。（**B**）の水泳プールは、「一日で失われたグリーンランドの110

億トンの氷床表面」が「水泳プール400万面分以上に相当」と言っているだけなので不正解。ニュースの最後で述べられている this season's ice melt has already raised global sea levels half a millimeter（今季の氷融解はすでに世界の海面水位を0.5ミリメートル上昇させている）と内容が一致する（**A**）が正解。

問題文 Worrying Temperatures in Greenland

Climate change is causing the ice to melt in Greenland in alarming amounts. Scientists say Greenland's ice sheet experienced its biggest melt of the summer on Thursday, losing 11 billion tons of surface ice to the ocean. That is equivalent to more than 4 million Olympic swimming pools, all gone in one day. Experts say because of recent heat waves in Europe and around the world, July was possibly the hottest month in recorded history. Greenland's ice sheet is the second largest in the world, and this season's ice melt has already raised global sea levels half a millimeter.

訳 グリーンランドの気がかりな気温

気候変動によって、グリーンランドで憂慮すべき量の氷が融解しています。科学者たちによれば、グリーンランドの氷床では木曜日にこの夏最大の融解が生じ、表面の110億トンの氷が（解けて）海に流れ出たということです。これはオリンピックの水泳プール400万面分以上に相当し、それがすべて一日で失われたのです。専門家によると、欧州や世界各地での最近の熱波が原因で、（2019年の）7月はおそらく観測史上最も暑い月だったとのことです。グリーンランドの氷床は世界第2位の大きさで、今季の氷融解はすでに世界の海面水位を0.5ミリメートル上昇させています。

語句

cause...to do: …が〜する原因となる ／ **melt:** ①〈氷な

どが〉解ける　②（氷の）融解／alarming: 憂慮すべき、気がかりな／amount: 量／ice sheet: （極地などの）氷床／lose A to B: AをBに取られて失う／be equivalent to: ～に相当する／heat wave: 熱波／sea level: 海面水位／

No.3　問題文 ⑯↓　設問 ⑰↓
オーストラリア英語

1.　正解 C

What is the main lesson that the couple should have learned?
(A) Keeping money is always better than spending it.
(B) You should never pay for an SUV with cash.
(C) You should not spend money that is not yours.

設問訳 この夫婦が学んだであろう主な教訓は何か。
(A) いかなる場合も、お金は使うより取っておいた方がいい。
(B) 決してSUVを現金で購入してはならない。
(C) 他人のお金を使ってはならない。

解説 lesson には「教訓」の意味があり、ニュースは Lesson learned, perhaps.（いい教訓になったことだろう）で締めくくられている。「銀行口座に誤って振り込まれたお金を使い込んだことで起訴された」という話から得られる教訓として最も自然なのは、(C) の「他人のお金を使ってはならない」だろう。(A) を選びそうになるかもしれないが、ニュースではお金を使うこと自体を戒めてはいない。SUVの支払い方法について話しているわけでもないので、(B) も不可。

2.　正解 B

What was the couple probably going to have to do?
(A) Make payments only by credit card
(B) Repay more than $100,000
(C) Tell their bank about the mistake

設問訳 この夫婦はその後どうする必要があったと思われるか。
(A) クレジットカードのみで支払う
(B) 10万ドル以上を返金する
(C) 銀行に間違いを伝える

解説 最後の方で述べられているhaving to pay more than 100 grand back to the bankを正しく聞き取ろう。主語は直前の they（＝ the couple）なので、「（夫婦は）10万ドル以上を銀行に返す必要がある」となる。pay backをrepayと言い換えた（B）が正解。

問題文　Couple Makes a Costly Mistake

A couple in the US learned the hard way the old saying "Finders keepers" isn't always true. Their bank accidentally put $120,000 into their account—money meant for someone else, of course. But instead of telling the bank about the mistake, the couple spent most of the cash on an SUV and camper, among other things. Now, they are facing felony-theft charges and having to pay more than 100 grand back to the bank. Lesson learned, perhaps.

訳　夫婦の高くついた誤り

米国のある夫婦は、「拾った人がその持ち主」という古いことわざは必ずしも正しいとは限らないということを身をもって知りました。彼らが利用する銀行が誤って彼らの口座に12万ドルを振り込みました。もちろん、それは別人（の口座）に振り込まれるはずのものでした。しかし夫婦はその手違いを銀行に伝えず、その現金の大半をSUVやキャンピングカーなどにつぎ込みました。現在、彼らは重窃盗罪で起訴され、10万ドル以上を銀行に返す必要が生じています。いい教訓になったことでしょう。

語句

costly: 大きな代償を伴う／learn the hard way（that）: つらい経験を通して～ということを学ぶ、～という厳しい現実を身をもって知る／saying: ことわざ／Finders keepers.: 拾った人がその持ち主　▶Finders keepers, losers weepers. とも。／accidentally: 誤って／account: 口座／(be) meant for: ～のためのものである、～用である／SUV: ＝ sport-utility vehicle　▶スポーツタイプの多目的車。／camper: キャンピングカー／among other things: 他のものとともに、とりわけ／face a...charge: …の罪で起訴される／felony: 重罪／theft: 窃盗／grand:《話》1000ドル／learn a lesson: 教訓を得る

Part 3 ニュース問題

1. 正解 C

What is the main problem that the women in the news report face?

(A) There is too much competition for a small number of jobs.

(B) They are expected to have a large number of children.

(C) They must work under harsh conditions without proper maternity care.

設問訳 このニュースに出てくる女性たちが直面している主な問題は何か。

(A) 少ない働き口をめぐる競争が激しすぎる。

(B) たくさん子どもを産むことを期待されている。

(C) 妊娠時に適切なケアを受けられずに、過酷な状況で働かなければならない。

語句 competition: 競争／harsh: 厳しい、過酷な

解説 (A) の「就業が困難である」という話や、(B) の「たくさん子どもを産むように言われている」といった話は出てこない。they don't get the care that they need（必要なケアを受けていない）／they collect leaves nine hours a day, six days a week（彼女らは1日9時間、週6日間、茶摘みに従事している）／The women say they get less money if they don't fill up their baskets.（この女性たちは、籠いっぱいに茶葉を摘まなければ、もらえるお金が減ると言っている）といった内容を要約した (C) が正解。

2. 正解 B

What does the news report say about the tea industry in Assam?

(A) Its workers enjoy India's highest standards of healthcare.

(B) Not all its plantations offer adequate medical care to workers.

(C) It exports tea through government agencies.

設問訳 このニュースは、アッサム州の紅茶業界についてどのように伝えているか。

(A) 労働者たちはインドの最高レベルの医療を受けている。

(B) すべてのプランテーションが労働者たちに十分な医療ケアを提供しているわけではない。

(C) 政府機関を通して紅茶を輸出している。

語句 adequate: 十分な

解説 The tea industry says it ensures that tea sold internationally meets the highest standards of health and labor protections（紅茶業界によれば、同業界は、世界で販売される茶葉が保健医療と労働者保護において最高水準を満たしたものであることを保証している）と述べられているため、(A) を選んでしまいそうになるが、その後に But at two unaccredited plantations... workers complained to CNN of a lack of medical care.（しかし、認定されていない2つのプランテーションでは……医療ケアが不十分だと労働者たちはCNNに訴えた）と述べられているので、正解は (B)。unaccredited の意味がわからなくても、But at two plantations で判断できるだろう。

3. 正解 C

What does the news report say about tea plantations in Assam?

(A) They pay workers by the hour.

(B) They don't employ pregnant women.

(C) Most of their workers are women.

設問訳 このニュースは、アッサム州の紅茶プランテーションについてどのように伝えているか。

(A) 労働者への支払いは時給制である。

(B) 妊娠している女性を雇用しない。

(C) そこで働いている労働者たちの大半は女性である。

解説 they collect leaves nine hours a day, six days a week（彼女らは1日9時間、週6日間、茶摘みに従事している）と「労働時間」について述べた箇所はあるが、時給制について述べた箇所はない。よって (A) は不適。また、冒頭で More than a million women, including some who are heavily pregnant, are employed to pick tea leaves（臨月の妊婦を含む100万人以上の女性が茶葉を摘み取るために雇用されている）と述べられているため、(B) も選べない。正解は (C) で、Assam has about 1.5 million tea-plantation workers. More than

70 percent of this workforce are women.（アッサム州では約150万人が紅茶プランテーションで働いている。その労働者たちの70％以上が女性だ）の言い換えになっている。

---

4. 正解 B

What does the reported comment by the health director imply?

(A) That Assam's maternal death rate will continue to rise

(B) That the state government already has a plan to improve the situation

(C) That nothing more can be done about the problem

設問訳 保健局長のコメントとして伝えられた内容が示唆していることは何か。

(A) アッサム州の妊産婦死亡率は今後も上昇し続ける

(B) 州政府はすでに状況を改善するための計画を立てている

(C) 問題に対してそれ以上できることは何もない

解説 Assam State still has a high maternal death rate: ...more than in any other state in India.（アッサム州では依然として妊産婦死亡率が高く……インドの他のどの州より高い）と伝えた後に、The state health director says the death rate is improving and he hopes things will continue to get better（州保健局長によると、死亡率は改善されてきており、状況が引き続き改善されることを期待しているということだ）と述べられているため、(A) は誤り。as they introduce new public-private partnerships with the plantations（プランテーションとの新たな官民連携の導入によって）という部分から、アッサム州では状況を改善するための計画を立てていることがわかるので、正解は (B)。

---

5. 正解 A

What is reported about female tea pickers in Assam?

(A) Some give birth in the fields where they work.

(B) They usually quit their jobs as soon as they become pregnant.

(C) They get a full day's pay when they take a day off to give birth.

設問訳 アッサム州の女性の茶摘みたちについて何と述べられているか。

(A) 働いている茶畑で出産する人もいる。

(B) 妊娠すると、たいていすぐに仕事を辞める。

(C) 出産のために一日休んだときは、丸1日分の給料がもらえる。

語句 quit: 〜を辞める／take a day off: 一日休みをとる

解説 最後の方で They work until the later stages of pregnancy and sometimes give birth in the fields.（彼女らは妊娠後期まで働き、時には茶畑で出産することもある）と述べられていることから、正解は (A)。「妊娠後期まで働く」と言っているので (B) は不正解。最後の部分で just can't afford to miss out on a full day's pay（とにかく丸1日分の稼ぎを逃すような経済的余裕もない）と述べられているので、(C) も内容にそぐわない。

問題文 **Tea Pickers Face Deep-Rooted Problem**

India's Assam State exports tea worth around $250 million a year, but it comes at a cost. More than a million women, including some who are heavily pregnant, are employed to pick tea leaves, and some of them say they don't get the care that they need.

Tucked away in the northeastern tip of India are the lush, green hills of Assam State. More than half of the country's tea leaves are grown in plantations here, but the bright vistas hide a dark reality.

Some female tea pickers get pregnant while working and feel that they have to stay in the plantations until they are full term. Temporary tea pickers who spoke to CNN said they collect leaves nine hours a day, six days a week. The women say they get less money if they don't fill up their baskets.

The tea industry says it ensures that tea sold internationally meets the highest standards of health and labor protections by working with independent accrediting agencies. But at two unaccredited plantations that CNN visited, workers complained to CNN of a lack of medical care.

"Assam has about 1.5 million tea-plantation workers. More than 70 percent of this workforce are women. These women [have] been working in the slave-like conditions for decades." (Jayshree Satpute, human-rights lawyer)

Since 2005, the Indian government has

introduced programs to provide free prenatal care—tests and births in public hospitals helping many people across the country. But Assam State still has a high maternal death rate: 237 women die per 100,000 births, more than in any other state in India. The state health director says the death rate is improving and he hopes things will continue to get better as they introduce new public-private partnerships with the plantations.

For now, though, many women don't have access to or are not aware of what services should be available to them. They work until the later stages of pregnancy and sometimes give birth in the fields. The women are afraid of what might happen, but just can't afford to miss out on a full day's pay.

訳　茶摘みをする人々が直面する根深い問題

インドのアッサム州は年間約2億5000万ドル相当の茶を輸出していますが、それには犠牲が伴っています。臨月の妊婦を含む100万人以上の女性が茶葉を摘み取るために雇用されていますが、中には必要なケアを受けていないと訴える人もいます。

インド北東端にひっそりと広がっているのは、アッサム州の緑豊かな丘陵です。国内の茶葉の半分以上がこの州のプランテーションで栽培されていますが、このまばゆい景色は暗い現実を隠しています。

茶摘みをする女性の中には、雇用期間中に妊娠しても、出産直前までプランテーションにいなければならないと感じる人もいます。CNNに話をしてくれた茶摘みの臨時労働者によると、彼女らは1日9時間、週6日間、茶摘みに従事しています。この女性たちは、籠いっぱいに茶葉を摘まなければ、もらえるお金が減るのだと言います。

（アッサム州の）紅茶業界によれば、同業界は独立した認定機関との協働によって、世界で販売される茶葉が保健医療と労働者保護において最高水準を満たしたものであることを保証しているということです。しかし、CNNが訪れた認定されていない2つのプランテーションでは、医療ケアが不十分だと労働者たちはCNNに訴えました。

「アッサム州では約150万人が紅茶プランテーションで働いています。その労働者たちの70％以上が女性です。この女性たちは数十年にわたり奴隷同然の状態で働いているのです」（ジャイシュリー・サトプテ　人権問題専門弁護士）

2005年以降、インド政府は出産前医療を無償で提供

するプログラムを導入しており、公立病院での検査や出産が可能となったことで、全国の大勢の人が恩恵を受けています。しかし、アッサム州では依然として妊産婦死亡率が高く、出産数10万件につき237人の女性が亡くなっています。これはインドの他のどの州より高い数値です。州保健局長によると、死亡率は改善されてきており、プランテーションとの新たな官民連携の導入によって状況が引き続き改善されることを期待しているということです。

とはいえ今のところ、多くの女性はそうしたサービスを利用できず、あるいは、どんなサービスが受けられるはずなのかを知りません。彼女らは妊娠後期まで働き、時には茶畑で出産することもあります。女性たちは（そういう無理をするせいで）起こるかもしれないことを恐れていますが、とにかく丸1日分の稼ぎを逃すような経済的余裕もないのです。

語句

export: ～を輸出する／worth: ～の価値がある／come at a cost: 大きな代償を伴う／be heavily pregnant: 出産間近である／employ: ～を雇用する／（be) tucked away: 旅行者があまり行かない場所にある／tip: 端／lush: 植物が青々と茂った／vista: 景色、眺め／full term: 臨月の、出産間近の／temporary: 一時的な、臨時の／ensure that: ～ということを確実にする、保証する／meet a standard: 基準を満たす／accrediting agency: 認定機関／unaccredited: 認定されていない／complain to A of B: AにB（苦痛・病苦など）を訴える／workforce: 全労働人口／slave: 奴隷／prenatal: 出産前の／maternal death rate: 妊産婦死亡率／public-private partnership: 官民連携／have access to: ～を利用できる／be aware of: ～を知っている／be available to: （主語を）～が利用できる／give birth: 出産する／can't afford to do: ～する経済的余裕がない／miss out on: ～を逃がす

1. 正解 A

What is the news report mainly about?
(A)Growing concern about e-cigarettes
(B)The need for more funding to fight an epidemic
(C)The policy of Juul Labs

設問訳 このニュースは主に何について述べているか。
(A) 電子たばこへの懸念の高まり
(B) 伝染病撲滅のための資金増加の必要性
(C) ジュール・ラブズ社の方針

解説 冒頭の It needs to be thought of as an injury to the lungs caused by something in the vaping, and it is very severe.（それは電子たばこの喫煙に伴う何かによる肺の損傷と考えられるべきで、非常に深刻なものだ）からニュースの最後まで、sounding the alarm や worry exploding などの表現を使って、電子たばこへの注意喚起や懸念について述べられている。よって、正解は（A）。epidemic には「伝染病」の意味もあるが、ここで使われているのは an epidemic of vaping（電子たばこのまん延）である。

2. 正解 C

What caused many people to worry?
(A)A large donation by the Bloomberg charity
(B)A surge in e-cigarette advertising
(C)A sudden increase in cases of lung illness

設問訳 多くの人の懸念を引き起こしたのは何か。
(A) ブルームバーグ基金からの多額の寄付
(B) 電子たばこ広告の急増
(C) 肺疾患患者の急増

語句 donation: 寄付 / surge in: 〜の急増

解説 ニュースの中で、Why is the worry exploding now?（なぜ今、[電子たばこへの] 懸念が爆発的に広まっているのか）という疑問の答えとして the Centers for Disease Control reported a huge jump in the number of people developing mysterious lung illnesses after vaping（米疾病対策センターの報告によると、電子たばこの使用後に原因不明の肺疾患を発病した患者数が急増し……）と述べられていることから、正解は（C）。

3. 正解 A

What was Juul Labs warned about?
(A)Giving people the wrong impression about its products
(B)Putting additives into its e-cigarettes
(C)Targeting nicotine users

設問訳 ジュール・ラブズ社は、何に関して警告を受けたか。
(A) 自社製品について人々に間違った印象を与えること
(B) 自社の電子たばこに添加物を入れること
(C) ニコチン使用者をターゲットにすること

解説 the Food and Drug Administration has warned Juul Labs, the leading manufacturer, about misleading advertising and statements（米食品医薬品局は電子たばこメーカー大手のジュール・ラブズ社に対し、誤解を招く広告や表現について警告している）と述べられており、これを「人々に間違った印象を与えること」と言い換えた（A）が正解。最後の方で if perhaps some additive is involved（もしかしたら何らかの添加物が関係しているのか）と述べた箇所はあるが、警告の内容ではないため（B）は不適。

4. 正解 B

What does the governor of New York probably think about e-cigarettes?
(A)That a ban on all smoking will solve the problem
(B)That more information about their safety is needed
(C)That the problem is not as serious as the media has reported

設問訳 ニューヨーク州知事は、電子たばこについておそらくどう考えているか。
(A) あらゆる喫煙を禁止することが問題を解決する
(B) 電子たばこの安全性についてより多くの情報が必要だ
(C) メディアが報じているほど問題は深刻ではない

解説 Juul says the company will fully cooperate with probes into their marketing and products.（ジュール社は、同社のマーケティングや商品に関する調査に全面的に協力するとしている）と、ジュール社の発言を紹介した後、But that's not enough for the governor of New

York, who is launching a state investigation（しかし、それはニューヨーク州知事にとっては十分でなく、知事は州の捜査に着手しようとしている）と述べられていることから、（**B**）が正解となる。

---

5. 正解 C

What caused the reported illnesses and deaths?

(**A**) Misleading advertising
(**B**) An additive
(**C**) The cause is still unclear.

設問訳 報告された病気や死をもたらしたのは何か。
(**A**) 誤解を招く広告
(**B**) ある添加物
(**C**) 原因はまだわかっていない。

解説 It is not clear yet how or even if vaping is definitively causing these illnesses or deaths, or if perhaps some additive is involved.（電子たばこがこうした［肺］疾患や死をどう引き起こしているのか、そもそもその明確な原因なのか、あるいは、もしかしたら何らかの添加物が関係しているのか、確かなことはまだわかっていない）と述べられていることから、not clear を unclear と言い換えた（**C**）が正解。

問題文　A Puzzling New Health Threat

"It needs to be thought of as an injury to the lungs caused by something in the vaping, and it is very severe." (Dr. David Persse, Houston Health Department)

In Houston, doctors are sounding the alarm as three people are hospitalized after using e-cigarettes. In New York, the Bloomberg charity is giving $160 million to fight what's being called an epidemic of vaping. Why is the worry exploding now? In just the past few days, the Centers for Disease Control reported a huge jump in the number of people developing mysterious lung illnesses after vaping, to over 450. At least a half dozen are believed to have died.

The American Medical Association has now come out urging people to avoid the use of all e-cigarette products. And the Food and Drug Administration has warned Juul Labs, the leading manufacturer, about misleading advertising and statements, especially to schoolkids, where vaping

is growing exponentially.

Juul says the company will fully cooperate with probes into their marketing and products.

"We never wanted any non-nicotine-user, and certainly nobody underage, to ever use Juul products." (James Monsees, Juul Labs cofounder)

But that's not enough for the governor of New York, who is launching a state investigation, complete with subpoenas.

"This is a frightening public-health phenomenon." (Andrew Cuomo, New York State governor)

It is not clear yet how or even if vaping is definitively causing these illnesses or deaths, or if perhaps some additive is involved. But many healthcare officials are clearly extremely worried and want to slam the brakes on this exploding industry while they sort it all out.

Tom Foreman, CNN, Washington.

訳　健康への不可解な脅威

「それは電子たばこの喫煙に伴う何かによる肺の損傷と考えられるべきで、非常に深刻なものです」（デービッド・パース医師　ヒューストン保健局）

ヒューストンでは、3人が電子たばこの使用後に入院したのを受けて、医師たちが注意を喚起しています。ニューヨークでは、ブルームバーグ基金がいわゆる電子たばこのまん延に対処すべく1億6000万ドルを提供しています。なぜ今、（電子たばこへの）懸念が爆発的に広まっているのか。米疾病対策センターの報告によると、ここ数日だけで電子たばこの使用後に原因不明の肺疾患を発病した患者数が急増し、450人以上にのぼったということです。少なくとも6人が死亡したとされています。

今ではアメリカ医師会があらゆる電子たばこ製品の使用を避けるよう表立って呼び掛けており、米食品医薬品局は電子たばこメーカー大手のジュール・ラブズ社に対し、誤解を招く広告や表現、特に電子たばこの使用が急増している学生たちに向けたものについて警告しています。

ジュール社は、同社のマーケティングや商品に関する調査に全面的に協力するとしています。

「われわれは、ニコチンを吸わない人や、当然いかなる未成年にも、ジュール社の製品を使ってほしいと思ったことは決してありません」（ジェームズ・モンシーズ　ジュール・ラブズ社共同創業者）

しかし、それはニューヨーク州知事にとっては十分でな

く、知事は召喚状も発せられる州の捜査に着手しようとしています。

「これは公衆衛生上の恐ろしい現象です」(アンドリュー・クオモ ニューヨーク州知事)

電子たばこがこうした(肺)疾患や死亡をどう引き起こしているのか、そもそもその明確な原因なのか、あるいは、もしかしたら何らかの添加物が関係しているのか、確かなことはまだわかっていません。しかし、医療当局者の多くは明らかにきわめて強い懸念を覚えており、この爆発的に拡大する業界に待ったをかけ、全容を解明したいと考えています。

CNNのトム・フォアマンがワシントンからお伝えしました。

語句

lung: 肺／vaping: 電子たばこを吸うこと／severe:〈病気などが〉深刻な、重症の／sound the alarm: 警鐘を鳴らす／be hospitalized: 入院する／e-cigarette: 電子たばこ／epidemic:(病気などの)流行、まん延／explode: 爆発的に増える、急増する／the Centers for Disease Control(and Prevention): 米疾病対策センター／develop:(病気に)かかる、なる／come out: 考えを明らかにする、表立った行動に出る／urge...to do:

…に〜するよう促す／avoid: 〜を避ける／the Food and Drug Administration: 米食品医薬品局／leading: 大手の／misleading: 誤解を招く／advertising: 広告／statement: 声明、公の場での発言／exponentially: 急激に／cooperate with: 〜に協力する／probe:(徹底的な)調査／underage: 未成年の／cofounder: 共同創業者／governor: 州知事／launch:(計画などを)開始する／investigation: 捜査、調査／complete with: 〜を備えた、〜付きの／subpoena: 召喚状／frightening: 恐ろしい、ぞっとするような／public-health: 公衆衛生の／phenomenon: 現象／definitively: 断定的に、間違いなく／additive: 添加物／extremely: 極度に／slam the brakes on: 〜に急ブレーキをかける／sort...out: …を解決する、解明する

Part 4 インタビュー問題

No.1

問題文 24↓ 設問 25↓

アメリカ英語(Fareed Zakaria)／**アメリカ英語**(Bill Gates)

1. 正解 B

What is the interview mainly about?
(**A**) Sanitation in slum areas
(**B**) Progress toward meeting global challenges
(**C**) Solutions to the problem of climate change

設問訳 このインタビューの主なテーマは何か。
(**A**) スラム街の公衆衛生
(**B**) 世界的な課題の解決に向けた進歩
(**C**) 気候変動問題の解決策

解説 インタビュアーは大きく分けて「トイレ・衛生問題」と「気候変動問題」についてゲイツ氏に質問している。そしてゲイツ氏は、それぞれの問題の進歩について語っているので、それらをまとめて表現している(**B**)が正解。

2. 正解 B

Why is it hard to introduce modern sewer systems into developing countries?
(**A**) Because people in those countries are not used to them
(**B**) Because the cost is too high for such countries
(**C**) Because such countries have very large populations

設問訳 開発途上国に現代の下水網を導入することが難しいのはなぜか。
(**A**) そうした国々の人々は、それに慣れていないから
(**B**) そうした国々にとって費用がかかりすぎるから
(**C**) そうした国々は人口が膨大だから

解説 ゲイツ氏がトイレについて語っているのは前半部分。the way we think of sanitation in the rich world is we build sewer systems, we put a lot of clean water in, and we build a processing plant. That is so expensive that these developing countries' cities won't have it.（富裕な世界の私たちが思い浮かべる公衆衛生方法といえば、下水網を構築し、大量の浄水を投入し、[下水]処理場を建てる、というものだ。しかし、それはあまりにもコストがかさむので、そうした開発途上国の都市に備わることはないだろう）と述べていることから、（**B**）が正解。

---

3. 正解 A

How is human waste treated in the newly developed toilets?

(**A**) It is burned.

(**B**) It is flushed away in clean water.

(**C**) It is buried in ash.

設問訳 人間の排せつ物は新しく開発されたトイレでどのように処理されるのか。

（A）燃やされる。

（B）浄水に流される。

（C）灰に埋められる。

語句 treat: 〜を処理する／flush away: 〜を水で洗い流す／bury: 〜を埋める

解説 ゲイツ氏は、新しく開発したトイレの特長を、the new idea is that the toilet itself would essentially burn up the human waste...（新たなアイデアとしてあるのは、トイレそのものが実質的に排せつ物を燃やし……）と述べている。よって、（A）が正解。

---

4. 正解 B

What is a major problem with the newly developed toilets?

(**A**) They are not suitable for tourist areas.

(**B**) They are still too expensive.

(**C**) They cannot treat a large enough volume of waste.

設問訳 新しく開発されたトイレの主な問題点は何か。

（A）観光地には不向きである。

（B）まだ高すぎる。

（C）十分な量の排せつ物を処理することができない。

語句 be suitable for: 〜に向いている

解説 ゲイツ氏は、「排せつ物を燃やすトイレ」について説明した後に、「私たちは魔法のようなことができるトイレを作り上げた」と述べ、さらにThey are 10 times more

---

expensive than they'll need to be...と続けている。they＝toiletsなので「それらのトイレは目標額の10倍の価格だ」ということ。これに当てはまるのは（**B**）である。

---

5. 正解 C

What does Gates seem to think about the world's big problems?

(**A**) Nuclear war and pandemics are the biggest of them all.

(**B**) They will cause a rise in childhood death.

(**C**) We may solve them if the trend of progress continues.

設問訳 ゲイツ氏は世界の大きな問題についてどのように考えていると思われるか。

（A）核戦争と疾病の大流行が何より大きな問題である。

（B）子どもの死亡者数増加の原因となるだろう。

（C）進歩の傾向が続けば、私たちはそれらの問題を解決するかもしれない。

解説 「核戦争」や「疾病の大流行」はThere's many things that we as humans should be worried about and think about...（私たちが人類全体として懸念すべき、考えるべきことは山ほどある）の具体例であるが、（A）の「何より大きな問題」とは言っていない。また、childhood death went from about 10 percent...we have it down to 5 percent globallyで、「子どもの死亡率は約10%から……それを世界的に5%まで下げた」と語られているので（B）も不適。it's a world of immense progress（世界はすさまじい進歩に満ちている）／you'd rather be born 20 years from now than today（今日生まれるより今から20年後に生まれた方がいい）などから、正解は（C）だと判断できる。

問題文 **The following is an interview with Microsoft founder Bill Gates.**

Fareed Zakaria You threw a...a party in Beijing, a toilet fair. Why are you obsessed with toilets?

Bill Gates I guess I'm obsessed. The challenge is that with the world urbanizing, and these developing countries, the biggest cities in the world will be places like Lagos—you know, 20, 30 million people. And the way we think of sanitation in the rich world is we build sewer systems, we put a lot of clean water in, and we build a processing plant.

That is so expensive that these developing countries' cities won't have it.

And so, whenever you tour a slum, you might smell or see that human waste is not being removed and...and processed. And so, the new idea is that the toilet itself would essentially burn up the human waste, turn it into ash and get rid of both the smell and the disease-causing nature of human waste. And that's the challenge we put to engineers seven years ago, and in Beijing, we showed how far we've come.

So, we have toilets that do this magic thing. They are 10 times more expensive than they'll need to be, but we're encouraged we'll get those out, sell them to places like tourist areas and use that volume, hopefully over the next five years, to get this $500 self-contained toilet.

Zakaria So, when you look at the problem of climate change... And as you said, to get to zero emissions involves a...revolutions in, you know, dozens and dozens of crucial parts of the world. You've got, you know, the problem of toilets. You've got massive urbanization. You've got the reality of...of Africa with all these young men. Doesn't it make...get you down? Doesn't it make you think these problems are insurmountable, they're so large?

Gates No, absolutely not. I mean, you have to remember the base case. We were all subsistence farmers, and on average, people lived to about age 30. And, you know, then as energy came along, [the] industrial revolution and, you know, the digital revolution and, you know, the understanding of biology, life has improved dramatically. And, you know, so childhood death went from about 10 percent before our foundation got going. Now, with our partners, we have it down to 5 percent globally—children [who] die before the age of five. So that's 6 million children a year who survive that were not surviving as recently as 1990.

So, you know, I see incredible progress. Yes, you know, you can worry about nuclear war or pandemics, you know, the AI takeover, polarization. There's many things that we as humans should be worried

about and think about, OK, how do we minimize that risk or adapt to that problem, including climate change. And, you know, I've probably put more investments into these various innovations, including better seeds, to help with the adaptation piece. Because we will have warming; even if things go perfectly, there's a lot more warming coming between now and the end of the century.

So, you know, it's a world of immense progress. And you'd rather be born today—you know, if you're a woman, a gay person, a person who gets a disease, you'd rather be born today than 20 years ago, and, you know, I...I feel very strongly you'd rather be born 20 years from now than...than today.

訳 **マイクロソフト創業者、
ビル・ゲイツ氏のインタビューです。**

ファリード・ザカリア あなたは北京でパーティーを開きましたね、トイレのフェアを。なぜあなたはトイレにこだわるのですか。

ビル・ゲイツ 私はおそらくとりつかれていますね。何が課題かというと、世界中で、特に（先ほど話していた）開発途上国で都市化が進むなか、いずれ世界最大級の都市は（ナイジェリアの）ラゴスなどになるということです、人口2000万、3000万人規模となって。富裕な世界の私たちが思い浮かべる公衆衛生方法といえば、下水網を構築し、大量の浄水を投入し、（下水）処理場を建てる、というものです。しかし、それはあまりにもコストがかさむので、そうした開発途上国の都市に備わることはないでしょう。

ですから、スラム街を見て回ると、においや目で気づくかもしれません、人の排せつ物が放置されていたり未処理だったりするのをね。ですから、新たなアイデアとしてあるのは、トイレそのものが実質的に排せつ物を燃やし、それを灰にすることで、においや病気を引き起こす人糞の性質を除去してしまうというものです。これが7年前に私たちがエンジニアたちに与えた課題です。北京（の展示会）では、私たちの進展ぶりをご覧に入れました。

つまり、私たちは魔法のようなことができるトイレを作り上げたのです。それらのトイレは目標額の10倍の価格ですが、われわれはそれらを商品化して観光地などの場所に売り、それで得たお金を使って、できれば今後5年で、（目標の）500ドルの完全自律型トイレを開発できるだろうと思っています。

ザカリア　では、気候変動の問題についてですが、あなたが言ったように、（温室効果ガスの）排出量ゼロを実現するためには世界の何十もの重要な地域で革新が必要です。トイレの問題しかり、巨大な都市化しかり、あれだけ多くの若者たちのいるアフリカの現実しかり。これらの問題はあなたの気力をそぐことはないのですか。これほど巨大だと、これらの問題は解決不可能だと思うことはないのでしょうか。

ゲイツ　いえ、まったくそんなことはありません。（今の生活の）土台となった状況を思い出すべきです。かつては誰もが自給自足農民で、人々の平均寿命は30歳といったところでした。そして、その、それからエネルギー（技術）の誕生、産業革命、デジタル革命、（生物の）生態の理解があって、生活は劇的に向上しました。そして、私たちの財団が活動を開始する前は、子どもの死亡率は約10％でした。それが今は、私たちのパートナーとともに、それを世界的に5％まで下げたのです、5歳になる前に子どもたちが亡くなる率をね。つまり、年に600万人の子どもが生き延びるようになりました。つい1990年までは生き延びることができなかった数です。

　ですから、私に言わせれば、驚くべき進歩が見られます。たしかに、核戦争や疫病の大流行、AIに（仕事を）奪われること、分極化などを心配するのも当然です。私たちが人類全体として懸念すべき、考えるべきことは山ほどあります。よし、そのリスクをいかに最小化しようか、気候変動を含む問題にいかに適応しようか、といったね。私はこうしたさまざまなイノベーション、たとえば品種改良された種子などに、より多くの投資を行ってきたと思います、適応という部分で役立つように。というのも、温暖化は避けられないからです。すべて（の対策）が完璧にうまくいったとしても、今から今世紀末までに、今まで以上に温暖化が進みます。

　要するに、そうですね、世界はすさまじい進歩に満ちています。そして人は今日生まれた方がいいと言えます——その、もし女性やゲイの人、病気を抱えた人なら、20年前より今日生まれた方がいいですし、今日生まれるより今から20年後に生まれた方がいいと強く思いますね。

語句

fair: 博覧会、見本市　▶2018年11月に北京で開催されたReinvented Toilet Expoのこと。／**be obsessed with**: 〜にとりつかれている、〜で頭がいっぱいである／challenge: 課題、難題／urbanize: 都市化する／sanitation: 公衆衛生／sewer system: 下水網、下水設備／processing plant: 処理工場／tour: 〜を見て回る／smell: ①《smell that》〜ということをにおいで気づく ②におい／human waste: 人間の排せつ物／remove: 〜を除去する、片付ける／process: 〜を処理する／essentially: 本質的に、基本的に／burn up: 〜を完全に燃やす／ash: 灰／get rid of: 〜を取り除く、排除する／nature: 性質、特質／be encouraged (that): 〜ということになるだろうと心強く思う／volume: （生産・取引などの）量／self-contained: 必要なものを完備した、自律型の／get to zero emissions: （温室効果ガスの）排出量をゼロにする／involve: 〜を必要とする／revolution: 革新、革命的なこと／crucial: 重要な／massive urbanization: 大規模な都市化／get...down: …のやる気をくじく／insurmountable: 〈困難などが〉克服できない／subsistence farmer: 自給自足農民／come along: やって来る、現れる／the industrial revolution: 産業革命／biology: 生態／dramatically: 劇的に／foundation: 財団、基金／get going: 軌道に乗る、動き出す／nuclear war: 核戦争／pandemic: 世界的流行病／takeover: 乗っ取り、奪取／polarization: 二極分化、格差の拡大／minimize: 〜を最小化する／adapt to: 〜に適応する、順応する／seed: 種子、種／adaptation: 順応、適応／immense: 非常に大きな、多大な

No.2

問題文 ㉖　設問 ㉗

アメリカ英語(Fareed Zakaria)／イギリス英語(David Cameron)

1.　正解 **B**

What are the main opinions expressed by Cameron in this interview?

(**A**) The UK and the US disagree too much, and the Iran deal had to be replaced.

(**B**) UK-US teamwork is crucial, and the US should have stayed in the Iran deal.

(**C**) The UK-US relationship is traditional, and the Iran deal caused instability.

設問訳 このインタビューでキャメロン氏が示した主な見解は何か。

(**A**) 英国と米国は見解が異なりすぎている、そしてイラン合意は別のものに変えるべきだった。

(**B**) 英米の協力は重要である、そして米国はイラン合意にとどまるべきだった。

(**C**) 英米関係は伝統的なものだ、そしてイラン合意は不安定さをもたらした。

解説 インタビューの前半で、キャメロン氏は自身とトランプ大統領の見解が異なる点を挙げつつ、英米関係については we've got to find ways of working together （協力する方法を見つけるべきだ）や、I want the relationship to work whoever is the prime minister or whoever is the president（私が求めるのは、うまく機能する英米関係なのだ、首相が誰であれ、大統領が誰であれね）と語っている。また、後半で「イラン合意を離脱したアメリカは誤りを犯したと思うか」と聞かれ、「イラン合意は、イランを恒久的に核兵器保有から遠ざけておくためのもの」「きちんとした解決策もないまま実際に合意を離脱するのは、本当に、世界の安全性を高めるより損なうことになると思う」と語っており、（**B**）が正解だとわかる。

2. 正解 C

On what topic did Cameron say he agrees with Trump?

(**A**) Free trade

(**B**) Climate change

(**C**) Fighting terrorism

設問訳 キャメロン氏がトランプ氏と見解が一致していると述べたのは何の話題についてか。

(**A**) 自由貿易

(**B**) 気候変動

(**C**) テロとの戦い

解説 キャメロン氏はトランプ氏と意見が一致していない点について、I'm a believer in action to tackle climate change... I'm a believer in free trade, and he's taking quite a lot of quite protectionist steps.（私は気候変動対策を支持している……私は自由貿易の信奉者だが、彼はかなり保護主義的な政策をかなり多く取っている）と述べている。よって（**A**）（**B**）は選べない。let's start with some areas where we agree: the fight

against Islamist extremism and terrorism（われわれの見解が一致している領域から始めよう。たとえば、イスラム過激主義とテロリズムに対する戦いだ）と述べられていることから、正解は（**C**）。

3. 正解 A

What did Cameron say was the basic benefit of the Iran deal?

(**A**) It would make sure that Iran did not get nuclear weapons.

(**B**) It would keep Iran from supporting Islamist extremists.

(**C**) It would allow Iran to join NATO.

設問訳 キャメロン氏によれば、イラン合意の基本的な利点は何か。

(**A**) 確実にイランは核兵器を入手できなくなる。

(**B**) イランがイスラム過激派を支援できなくなる。

(**C**) イランがNATOに加盟することが可能になる。

語句 benefit: 利点／allow...to do: …が〜することを可能にする

解説 イラン合意の話題が出るのはインタビューの後半。イスラム過激派やNATOについて触れられているのはインタビューの前半で、イラン合意とは無関係。正解は（**A**）。what we managed to negotiate was to keep Iran permanently away from having a nuclear weapon...（とにかく、われわれが何とか成立させた合意は、イランを恒久的に核兵器保有から遠ざけておくためのものであり……）から判断できるだろう。

4. 正解 C

What did Cameron imply about the Iran deal he helped to negotiate?

(**A**) That it had too many imperfections

(**B**) That it could work only while Obama was president

(**C**) That it guaranteed at least some degree of certainty

設問訳 キャメロン氏が、自身が交渉に寄与したイラン合意について示唆したことは何か。

(**A**) 欠陥が多すぎた

(**B**) オバマ氏が大統領だった間のみ機能できた

(**C**) 少なくともある程度の情勢の安定を保証していた

語句 guarantee: 〜を保証する／certainty: 確実性

解説 米国のイラン合意離脱に触れて、キャメロン氏は

And the trouble with getting out of it is you're replacing something with huge uncertainty. (合意から離脱してしまえば、そのある程度効果のあるものに代わって［情勢の］大きな不確実性をもたらすことになる) と述べ、さらに、インタビューの最後で getting rid of that deal makes the situation more unsafe (この合意をなくすことは情勢をより不安定にする) と述べている。逆に言えば、「イラン合意は情勢の安定化に一役買っていた」ということなので、(**C**) が正解。

---

5. 正解 A

What view did Cameron say he shared with members of Congress?

(**A**) That Iran supports terrorist groups

(**B**) That Iran promotes stability in the Middle East

(**C**) That the West shouldn't expect Iran to be perfect

設問訳 キャメロン氏が米連邦議員と同じだと述べた見解は何か。

(**A**) イランはテロリスト集団を支援している

(**B**) イランは中東の安定を促進している

(**C**) 欧米諸国はイランに完璧さを期待すべきではない

解説 キャメロン氏は I share all the concerns of those in Congress and the president who say... (…と言う米連邦議会の議員たちや大統領の懸念を私も持っている) と述べており、say 以下で it support [s] terrorist groups (テロリスト集団を支援している) ということが挙げられている。it は、直前の Iran has a terrible record (イランはひどい行為を働いた過去がある) を受けた Iran の代名詞なので、正解は (**A**)。

問題文 **The following is an interview with former British prime minister David Cameron.**

Fareed Zakaria   David, you've seen a lo...lot of politicians in action. What do you make of Donald Trump?

David Cameron   Well, there are not many areas where we agree, on the face of things. I'm a believer in action to tackle climate change; I'm not sure he is. I'm a staunch defender of NATO, and he said in the past it might be obsolete. I'm a believer in free trade, and he's taking quite a lot of quite protectionist steps. But I think...I believe so much in the

special relationship between Britain and the United States that we've got to find ways of working together. So let's start with some areas where we agree: the fight against Islamist extremism and terrorism.

Zakaria   He's done something extraordinary, though, in wading into British politics. When Boris Johnson was not prime minister, he openly and loudly supported him, kept talking about how he'd be good. Why...why do you think he finds that commonality?

Cameron   Well, I think, interestingly, both of them are...are quite establishment figures and yet sort of raging against the establishment. They obviously have some commonality, and there are some similarities in what happened with the Brexit vote and what happened with the election of Donald Trump in...in...in 2016.

But, look, I want the relationship to work whoever is the prime minister or whoever is the president. I mean, Donald Trump does go about politics in a totally different way, and people like me who are perhaps a bit more traditional about things you'd say about other people's election campaigns and all the rest of it—we have to recognize maybe some of the rules are changing.

Zakaria   Final thoughts, on Iran. You were there when the Iran deal was negotiated. Do you think that the Americans made a mistake by pulling out of it?

Cameron   Well, I do, because, look, it...it's certainly right to say the deal had its imperfections, but all deals have their imperfections. But fundamentally, what we managed to negotiate—and I think it was a great credit to President Obama, all the work that he did—what we managed to negotiate was to keep Iran permanently away from having a nuclear weapon, with the right to inspect and verify that that was the case. And the trouble with getting out of it is you're replacing something with huge uncertainty. By all means, try and improve on the deal, try and make sure that it runs on for longer...longer, but actually walking away from it without a real answer, I think, actually makes the world less safe rather than more safe.

Zakaria Are you worried that there might be actual conflict in the Middle East?

Cameron Well, I worry that it's a very dangerous situation. And, of course, I share all the concerns of those in Congress and the president who say that Iran has a terrible record, that it support[s] terrorist groups, that it is an author of instability. I buy… share all of those arguments. But often in politics and international affairs, we're not dealing with perfection, and we're not dealing with a choice that is brilliant against a choice that is terrible; we're dealing with a set of, you know, often poor choices, but you pick the best one you can, and that's what I think our deal did, and getting rid of that deal makes the situation more unsafe.

訳　デービッド・キャメロン元英国首相の インタビューです。

ファリード・ザカリア デービッド、あなたは大勢の政治家の働きぶりを見てきました。ドナルド・トランプ氏についてどう思いますか。

デービッド・キャメロン そうですね、一見したところ、私と彼の意見が一致している領域は多くありません。私は気候変動対策を支持しています。彼は支持しているとは言い難い。私は筋金入りのNATO擁護者ですが、彼は以前、NATOは時代遅れではないかと発言しました。私は自由貿易の信奉者ですが、彼はかなり保護主義的な政策をかなり多く取っています。しかし思うに……私は英米間の特別な関係を固く信じていますから、協力する方法を見つけるべきだと思います。ですから、われわれの見解が一致している領域から始めましょう。たとえば、イスラム過激主義とテロリズムに対する戦いです。

ザカリア しかし、トランプ氏は驚くべきこともしましたよね、イギリス政界に干渉するという。ボリス・ジョンソン氏がまだ首相でなかった頃にトランプ氏は、公に、声高にジョンソン氏を支持し、彼がいかにすぐれた首相になるかということを何度も言っていました。なぜ大統領は（ジョンソン氏との）共通点を見いだしているのだと思い

ますか。

キャメロン そうですね、私が思うに、興味深いのは、彼らは2人ともほとんど体制側の人間でありながら、体制に対して憤ってもいます。彼らには明らかに共通点がいくつかあり、2016年のEU離脱をめぐる投票で起きたこととドナルド・トランプ氏の当選で起きたことにもいくつかの類似点があります。

　ただですね、私が求めるのは、うまく機能する英米関係なのです、首相が誰であれ、大統領が誰であれね。その、ドナルド・トランプ氏は確かにまったく違う形で政治を進めますよね。そして、私のような、他人の選挙活動やら何やらについて言うべきことに関して、おそらく（トランプ氏に比べて）もう少し従来の考え方をする人間は、物事のルールが一部変化しつつあるかもしれないことを認めなければなりませんね。

ザカリア 最後に伺いたいのはイランのことです。イラン合意の交渉時、あなたはその当事者の一人でした。その合意を離脱したアメリカは誤りを犯したと思いますか。

キャメロン ええ、そう思います、なぜなら、いいですか、確かにあの合意には欠陥があったと言えます。しかし、どんな合意にも欠陥はあるものです。それでも根本的に、われわれが苦労してまとめ上げた合意──ところで私は、あれはオバマ大統領の立派な功績だったと思います、彼の成したすべてがね──とにかく、われわれが何とか成立させた合意は、イランを恒久的に核兵器保有から遠ざけておくためのものであり、視察し、それ（核を保有していないということ）が事実であることを確かめる権利が含まれていました。合意から離脱してしまえば、そのある程度効果のあるものに代わって（情勢の）大きな不確実性をもたらすことになります。もちろん、その合意がより良いものになるように、確実により長く機能するように努力してほしいのですが、きちんとした解決策もないまま実際に合意を離脱するというのは、本当に、世界の安全性を高めるより損なうことになると私は思いますね。

ザカリア 中東で実際に戦争が勃発するかもしれないという懸念はありますか。

キャメロン そうですね、非常に危うい情勢であると懸念しています。もちろん、米連邦議会の議員たちや大統領の言う懸念を私も持っています。つまり、イランはひどい行為を働いた過去がある、テロリスト集団を支援してい

る、情勢不安の元凶だ、などというね。それはわかります……そうした主張については同感です。ただ政治や国際問題においてはよくあることですが、私たちが扱うのは必ずしも完璧なものではありません。素晴らしい選択肢とひどい選択肢のどちらかを選ぶ、といったことでもありません。われわれが扱っているのは一連の、その、しばしばパッとしない選択肢ばかりで、だとしてもその中で一番マシなものを選ぶわけです。われわれの合意はまさにそれだったと思いますし、この合意をなくすことは情勢をより不安定にしますよ。

語句

in action: 活動中の／What do you make of...?: …をどう思いますか／on the face of things: 一見したところ、表面上は／believer in: ～の信奉者、支持者／tackle: ～に対処する、取り組む／staunch: 忠実な、断固たる／defender of: ～の擁護者／obsolete: 古くさい、時代遅れの／protectionist: 保護主義的な／Islamist extremism: イスラム過激主義／extraordinary: 驚くべき、異常な／wade into: ～に干渉する／commonality: 共通性、共通点／establishment: ①体制の、支配者層の ②《the～》体制、支配者層／figure: 人物、(特に)著名な人／rage against: ～に対して激しく怒る／similarity: 類似点／Brexit: イギリスのEU離脱／work: 機能する／go about: ～に取り組む／and all the rest of it: その他もろもろ／recognize: ～を認める／the Iran deal: イラン合意 ➤2015年7月、イランと米英仏独中ロが結んだ核合意。イランが核開発を制限し、その見返りにイランに対する経済制裁を徐々に解除していくというもの。'18年5月に米国が合意を離脱し、

イランへの制裁を再開したことで、イランは合意の一部履行を停止すると宣言した。／negotiate: 交渉して～を取り決める／pull out of: ～を脱退する、離脱する／imperfection: 不完全さ、欠点／fundamentally: 根本的に、基本的に／manage to do: 何とか～する／be a credit to: ～の功績である、手柄である／keep A away from B: AをBに近づけない／permanently: 恒久的に／nuclear weapon: 核兵器／inspect: 詳しく調べる／verify that: ～が事実であると確かめる／be the case: 真実である／replace A with B: AをBと取り替える／uncertainty: 不安定さ、不確かさ／by all means: ぜひとも、もちろん／improve on: ～を改善する／run on: 続く、継続する／walk away from: ～から手を引く、抜ける／conflict: 戦争、紛争／Congress: (米国の)連邦議会／record: 経歴、履歴／author of: ～の張本人／instability: 不安定な状態／buy: ～を信じる、受け入れる／argument: 主張／international affairs: 国際情勢、国際問題／perfection: 完全なこと／brilliant: 見事な、優れた／a set of: 一連の／get rid of: ～を取り除く、なくす

Reading Section リーディング編

Part 1 語彙問題

No.1

正解 A

Two minke whales became the first <u>casualties</u> on the day Japan officially resumed commercial whaling for the first time in 30 years.
(**A**) casualties (**B**) detriments (**C**) offerings

訳

日本が商業捕鯨を30年ぶりに公式に再開した日、2頭のミンククジラがその最初の犠牲となりました。

語句

minke whale: ミンククジラ／casualty: 犠牲者、死傷者／officially: 公式に、正式に／resume: ～を再開する／commercial whaling: 商業捕鯨／detriment: 損

害、損失／ offering: 提供されるもの

No.2

正解 B

Jewels belonging to Marie Antoinette have **fetched** a queen's ransom at auction.
(**A**) accorded　(**B**) fetched　(**C**) sought

訳

マリー・アントワネットが所有していた宝石が、オークションで高値で売れました。

語句

fetch: （ある値段で）売れる／ a queen's ransom: 大金 ►「女王が人質として捕らわれたときに支払う身代金」から。a king's ransom がより一般的。／ accord: 〜を与える、授ける／ seek: 〜を求める ►過去形は sought。

No.3

正解 C

More than 70 years after the Holocaust, there are a/an **dwindling** few survivors to pass on their memories.
(**A**) abating　(**B**) dispersing　(**C**) dwindling

訳

ホロコーストから70年以上がたち、その記憶を伝える数少ない生存者たちも減り続けています。

語句

dwindling: 徐々に減少している／ survivor: 生き残った人、生存者／ pass on: 〜を伝える、伝達する／ abate: 〈勢いなどが〉衰える、〈痛みなどが〉和らぐ／ disperse: 散らばる、分散する

No.4

正解 A

The president turned his **back** on climate commitments in the name of jobs and economic growth.
(**A**) back　(**B**) head　(**C**) palm

訳

大統領は、雇用や経済成長のためとして、気候変動に関する約束を放棄しました。

語句

turn one's back on: 〜を見放す、放棄する／ commitment: 約束、言質／ in the name of: 〜のために、〜という名目で／ palm: 手のひら

Part 2　短文読解問題

No.1

1.　正解 B

What is the main point of the news report?
(**A**) That robots cannot spot mistakes as well as humans can
(**B**) That not all workforce robots take humans' jobs
(**C**) That robots make more mistakes than humans do

設問訳 このニュースの主旨は何か。
(**A**) ロボットは人間ほどミスを発見することができない
(**B**) すべての労働ロボットが人間の職を奪うわけではない
(**C**) ロボットは人間よりもミスを犯す

解説 後半部分に These coworking robots...can spot mistakes that humans overlook（こうした協働ロボットたちは……人間が見落とすミスを発見できる）とあるので、（**A**）は不正解。また、ロボットと人間のミスの数を比較した箇所はないので（**C**）も誤り。「今後数年のうちに数百万の職がロボットに奪われる」という世界経済フォーラムの概算を紹介しつつ、SEW says using robots...which means it can hire more human workers.（SEW 社によれば、ロボットを利用することで……結果として人間の労働者の雇用増につながっている）と述べているので、正解は（**B**）となる。

2. 正解 C

According to SEW, what has using robots enabled the company to do?

(**A**) Replace most of its workers with robots

(**B**) Give its human workers some much-needed time off

(**C**) Create more jobs for people

設問訳 SEW 社によると、ロボットを利用することで同社は何ができるようになったか。

(**A**) ほとんどの従業員をロボットに代える

(**B**) 人間の労働者に待望の休みを与える

(**C**) 人間の雇用をより多く生み出す

解説 at German manufacturer SEW Eurodrive, robots are there to cooperate with humans, not replace them（ドイツのメーカー、SEW オイロドライブでは、ロボットは人間に取って代わるのではなく、人間と共に働くものとしてある）とあるので、(**A**) は不正解。(**B**) の休みについては述べられていない。SEW says using robots…which means it can hire more human workers. から、(**C**) が正解だとわかる。

問題文 Rethinking Workplace Robots

Robots are an increasingly common part of the manufacturing workforce. In Germany, for example, Volkswagen uses robots to manufacture cars. Robots seem to be competing with humans for jobs, and the World Economic Forum estimates that millions of jobs will be lost to robots in the next few years.

However, at German manufacturer SEW Eurodrive, robots are there to cooperate with humans, not replace them. These coworking robots ("cobots") do heavy manual labor, deliver parts and can spot mistakes that humans overlook. SEW says using robots allows the company to be more productive and expand its operations, which means it can hire more human workers.

訳 労働ロボットを見直す

ロボットは製造業の労働力の一部としてますます普及しつつあります。たとえばドイツでは、フォルクスワーゲンが車の製造にロボットを使っています。ロボットは人間と職を奪い合っているように見え、世界経済フォーラムの概算では、今後数年のうちに数百万の職がロボットに奪われるとしています。

しかし、ドイツのメーカー、SEW オイロドライブでは、ロボットは人間に取って代わるのではなく、人間と共に働くものとしてあります。こうした協働ロボット（コボット）たちは、重労働を担い、部品を運搬し、さらには人間が見落とすミスを発見することができます。SEW 社によれば、ロボットを利用することで、同社は以前より生産性を上げたり、事業を拡大したりすることが可能になり、結果として人間の労働者の雇用増につながっているということです。

語句

common: よくある／manufacturing: 製造業の／workforce: 労働力／manufacture: ～を製造する／compete with A for B: BをめぐってAと競合する／estimate that: ～だと見積もる、概算する／replace: ～に取って代わる／heavy manual labor: 重労働／deliver: ～を届ける／spot: ～を発見する／overlook: ～を見逃す、見落とす／allow…to do: …が～することを可能にする／productive: 生産力のある／operation: 事業／hire: ～を雇用する

No.2

1. 正解 A

What is the news report mainly about?

(**A**) A welcome refuge amid war

(**B**) A place where rebels held secret meetings

(**C**) A change in the control of Darayya

設問訳 このニュースは主に何について述べているか。

(**A**) 戦時中のありがたい避難所

(**B**) 反政府軍が秘密の会合を開いた場所

(**C**) ダラヤの支配権の移行

語句 welcome: ありがたい、喜ばしい／amid: ～の最中に、真っただ中に

解説 冒頭の A secret library in Syria was once a place of comfort and refuge…（シリアのとある秘密の図書館は、かつて癒やしと避難の場所で……）や、最後の the library was only a memory in the minds of Amjad and the other former residents（その図書館はアムジャド君ら元住民たちの心の中の思い出として存在するのみとなっていた）から、このニュースは、シリアの

内戦中に地元住民が避難場所としていた図書館について述べたものだとわかる。よって、正解は（**A**）。

---

2. 正解 C

Who was in control of Darayya from August 2016?

(**A**) Rebel soldiers

(**B**) A 14-year-old boy

(**C**) The Syrian government

設問訳 2016年8月からダラヤを支配したのは誰か。

(**A**) 反政府軍の兵士たち

(**B**) 14歳の少年

(**C**) シリア政府

解説 The rebels made a deal with the government in August 2016, agreeing to hand over control of Darayya（反政府軍は2016年8月にシリア政府と取引を行い、ダラヤの支配権を譲渡することに合意した）と述べられていることから、正解は（**C**）。

問題文 A Special Place Now Lost

A secret library in Syria was once a place of comfort and refuge where local residents, especially children, escaped the horrors of war around them and found solace among books. The chief librarian was a 14-year-old boy named Amjad, who was in charge of everything and spent many hours there.

The library was in Darayya, a suburb of Damascus, which was besieged by Syrian-government forces for nearly four years while rebels were in control of the area. The rebels made a deal with the government in August 2016, agreeing to hand over control of Darayya in exchange for safe passage out of the area. After the handover, Syrian-government soldiers took control of the town, and all the civilians were relocated to other areas. By then, Darayya had been completely destroyed, and the library was only a memory in the minds of Amjad and the other former residents.

訳 今はなき特別な場所

シリアのとある秘密の図書館は、かつて癒やしと避難の場所で、地元住民、特に子どもたちが、彼らを取り巻く戦争の悲惨さから逃れ、本の中に安らぎを見いだしていました。図書館長はアムジャドという14歳の少年で、そこでのあらゆる仕事を担当し、何時間もそこで過ごしていました。

その図書館は、ダマスカス郊外のダラヤにありました。この地は反政府軍の実効支配下にあった間、4年近くにわたってシリア政府軍に包囲されていました。反政府軍は2016年8月にシリア政府と取引を行い、その地を安全に抜け出すのと引き換えに、ダラヤの支配権を譲渡することに合意しました。譲渡後、シリア政府軍の兵士らがこの町を掌握し、全市民が別の地域に移住させられました。そのときには、ダラヤはすでに完全に破壊され、その図書館はアムジャド君ら元住民たちの心の中の思い出として存在するのみとなっていました。

語句

comfort: 癒やし、慰め／refuge: 保護、避難／local resident: 地元住民／escape: ～を逃れる／horrors: 惨事、悲惨さ／solace: 慰め、安らぎ／chief librarian: 図書館長／be in charge of: ～を担当している、～の責任者である／besiege:〈軍が〉(敵地を)包囲する／rebels: 反政府勢力、反乱軍／make a deal with: ～と取引する、協定を結ぶ／hand over: ～を譲渡する／in exchange for: ～と引き換えに／safe passage out of: ～からの安全な脱出／handover: (領土・権利などの)譲渡／take control of: ～を支配下に置く、統制する／civilian: 一般市民、非軍人／relocate A to B: AをBに移住させる

No.3

---

1. 正解 A

What is the news report mainly about?

(**A**) A humanitarian crisis in Mexico

(**B**) Mexico's policy toward the United States

(**C**) Economic development in Central America

設問訳 このニュースは主に何について述べているか。

(**A**) メキシコにおける人道危機

(**B**) メキシコの対米政策

(**C**) 中米の経済開発

解説 第1段落でBut their rising number, as well as changes in policy about them, have led to a humanitarian crisis.（しかし、そうした移民の増加と、彼らに対する政策の変更が、人道危機を生み出した）と述べられ、第2段落で「移民の増加により、メキシコ政府が短期ビ

ザの発給数を減らしたことで、多くの人が不法滞在のままとなっている」ことがわかる。よって、正解は（A）。

2. 正解 B

Why have many of the migrants been unable to reach their goal?

（A）Because they have run out of money and must stay and work in Mexico

（B）Because it has become more difficult to enter the United States

（C）Because they have become separated from the caravans

設問訳 なぜ移民の多くが目的を達成できていないのか。

（A）資金が尽きたため、メキシコに滞在して働かなくてはならないから

（B）米国への入国がより難しくなったから

（C）キャラバンとはぐれてしまったから

語句 run out of: 〜がなくなる、尽きる／become separated from: 〜とはぐれる

解説 設問の reach their goal とは、冒頭文の with the goal of entering the United States から「米国に入国すること」だとわかる。移民が米国に入国できないのは、第2段落で Meanwhile, the United States has made it harder for the migrants to cross the US border, leaving many stuck in Mexico without visas or jobs.（一方、米国は、移民が米国との国境を越えるのをより困難にしており、多くの人がビザも仕事もないままメキシコにとどまっている）と述べられているように、（B）の「米国への入国がより難しくなったから」である。

問題文　Delicate Dilemma for Mexico

Mexico has many migrants, most from Central America, traveling through the country in caravans with the goal of entering the United States. But their rising number, as well as changes in policy about them, have led to a humanitarian crisis.

The Mexican government had previously promised a more humane approach to the migrants and started granting temporary visas to some of them. But then it realized that it could not sustain the growing migrant population and reduced the number of visas it granted, leaving many people undocumented. Meanwhile, the United States has made it harder for the migrants to cross the US border, leaving many stuck in Mexico without visas or jobs.

The United States is also putting pressure on Mexico to limit migration into Mexico from the south. Mexico plans to boost economic development in its southern areas and in Central America as a way to reduce the number of migrants moving through the country.

訳　メキシコの解決困難なジレンマ

メキシコには多くの移民がいますが、ほとんどが中米から来た人たちで、彼らはキャラバンを組んでメキシコを通り、米国へ入国することを目指しています。しかし、そうした移民の増加と、彼らに対する政策の変更が、人道危機を生み出しました。

メキシコ政府はそれ以前に、より人道的な移民対策をとると約束し、短期ビザを一部の人に発給し始めていました。しかし、その後、増加する移民を支えるのは無理だと気づき、発給するビザの数を減らしたことで、多くの人が不法滞在のままとなっています。一方、米国は、移民が米国との国境を越えるのをより困難にしており、多くの人がビザも仕事もないままメキシコにとどまっています。

米国はまた、南からのメキシコへの入国を制限するようメキシコ政府に圧力をかけています。メキシコ政府は、同国南部および中米の経済開発を促進することで、同国を通過する移民の数を減らそうと計画しています。

語句

delicate: 慎重を要する、微妙な／migrant: 移民、移住者／caravan:（旅人の）一行、キャラバン／lead to: 〜をもたらす、引き起こす／humanitarian crisis: 人道危機／previously: 以前に／humane: 人道的な、人情のある／grant A to B: AをBに与える／temporary visa: 一時ビザ、短期滞在の在留資格／sustain:（生命・生活などを）支える、維持する／reduce: 〜を減らす／leave A B: AをBの状態にしておく／undocumented: 不法滞在の／(be) stuck in: 〜で立ち往生している／limit: 〜を制限する／migration into: 〜への移住／boost: 〜を後押しする、押し上げる

Part 3 長文読解問題

No.1

1. 正解 C

What is the main topic of the news report?
(A) The birth of a cow at the International Space Station
(B) The environmental footprint of the traditional meat industry
(C) Technology to grow meat outside of animals

設問訳 このニュースの主旨は何か。
(A) 国際宇宙ステーションでの牛の誕生
(B) 従来の食肉産業の環境負荷
(C) 動物の体外で肉を育てる技術

解説 第1段落の commercially producing slaughter-free, ecofriendly meat（屠殺を伴わない、環境にやさしい肉の商用生産）、第2段落の put them in an artificial environment mimicking the inside of a cow's body（牛の体内を模した人工的な環境に入れる）、最終段落の develop in vitro or "clean" meat（試験管肉、つまり「クリーン」ミートの開発）といった表現から、(C) が正解。

2. 正解 A

What is needed to begin growing steaks by the method Aleph Farms uses?
(A) Cells from a cow
(B) Connective muscle tissue
(C) An artificial environment for cows

設問訳 アレフ・ファームズが使用している方法でステーキ用肉を育て始めるのに必要なものは何か。
(A) 牛の細胞
(B) 結合筋組織
(C) 牛用の人工的な環境

解説 第2段落の Here's how it works. Researchers take cells from a cow,...（しくみは次の通り。研究者が牛から細胞を採取し……）や、第6段落の the cell-based process（この細胞を使う工程）から、正解は (A) となる。

3. 正解 A

What does the news say is one of the merits of the new meat technology?

(A) It could improve global food security.
(B) It would create many new jobs.
(C) It would allow more cows to be used for milk instead of meat.

設問訳 このニュースによると、新しい食肉技術の利点の1つは何か。
(A) 世界的な食料の安定確保を向上させるかもしれない。
(B) 多くの新たな雇用を創出することができるだろう。
(C) より多くの牛を食肉用ではなく乳用に使うことができるだろう。

解説 第4段落で、3Dバイオプリンティング・ソリューションズの言葉として、The space-grown meat could help... address food insecurity among the booming population down on Earth（この宇宙育ちの肉は……地球上で人口が爆発的に増えていくなかで食料不安の対処法にもなりうる）と紹介されている。また、第7段落で、「今回の合同実験は、来るべき世代のために食料を安定的に確保するという私たちのビジョンの達成に向けた、大きな初めの一歩」というアレフ・ファームズのトゥビアCEOの発言があることから、(A) が正解。

4. 正解 B

What does the Aleph Farms CEO imply about conventional meat farming?
(A) Its products taste better than cell-based meat.
(B) It is inhumane.
(C) It produces more nutritious meat.

設問訳 アレフ・ファームズのCEOが従来の畜産業について示唆していることは何か。
(A) 製品は細胞を使った肉よりおいしい。
(B) 非人道的である。
(C) より栄養価の高い肉を生み出している。
語句 inhumane: 非人道的な、残酷な／nutritious: 栄養のある

解説 第5段落で、アレフ・ファームズの新しい肉の生産方法について、「ただステーキ用肉を生み出すためのマシンにすぎないものとして」牛を用いることに代わる、より優れた選択肢だというトゥビアCEOの言葉が紹介されている。また、第6段落に The company says that the cell-based process is not only more humane...（同社によれば、この細胞を使う工程はより人道的なだけでなく……）とあることから、CEOは従来の畜産業について

（**B**）のように思っていると考えられる。

---

5. 正解 C

How could switching to engineered steaks help the environment?

（**A**）More land could be used for raising pigs and poultry.

（**B**）It would reduce transportation-sector emissions.

（**C**）Fewer cows would mean lower greenhouse-gas emissions.

設問訳 人工的に作り出したステーキ用肉に変えることは、環境にどのように役立ちうるか。

（**A**）豚と家禽を育てるためにより多くの土地が使用されるかもしれない。

（**B**）輸送部門から出る排ガスを減らすことができるだろう。

（**C**）牛が少なくなることで温室効果ガスが減少するだろう。

解説 第6段落でBeef alone is responsible for 41 percent of livestock greenhouse-gas emissions,… That's more than direct emissions from the transportation sector.（牛肉だけで家畜による温室効果ガス排出量の41％を占めており……これは輸送部門からの直接的な排出量を上回る数値だ）と述べられている。つまり、人工的に牛肉を作り出せば牛を減らすことができ、その結果、温室効果ガスが減少しうると考えられるので、正解は（**C**）。

問題文 Starting a Revolution in Food

You may one day be able to eat burgers grown in space. Aleph Farms, an Israeli food company that engineers beef steaks from cow cells, has successfully grown meat on the International Space Station for the first time. This is a significant step toward the company's goal of commercially producing slaughter-free, ecofriendly meat.

Here's how it works. Researchers take cells from a cow, give them nutrients and put them in an artificial environment mimicking the inside of a cow's body. The cells then multiply, grow into connective muscle tissue and eventually become a full-sized steak. Aleph Farms collaborated with a Russian bioprinting company, 3D Bioprinting Solutions, to successfully carry out the process.

According to Aleph Farms, this cutting-edge research, conducted in some of the most extreme environments imaginable, indicates the growth potential of sustainable food-production methods that avoid the land waste, water waste and pollution that conventional beef production involves.

The space-grown meat could help feed astronauts during long-term manned space missions as well as address food insecurity among the booming population down on Earth, according to a statement by 3D Bioprinting Solutions. Aleph Farms says its products are not yet commercially available but will likely be ready for the market in three or four years.

Didier Toubia, CEO of Aleph Farms, told CNN that the factory-farming industry had "lost the connection with the animal" and that growing slaughter-free steaks was a better alternative to using cows "as mere machines to produce steaks."

The company says that the cell-based process is not only more humane but also better for the environment, one of its aims being to make meat with a minimal environmental footprint. Conventional beef production uses up a lot of land and resources. Cows grow and reproduce more slowly than pigs and poultry, so they eat a lot more and need more land and water. Beef alone is responsible for 41 percent of livestock greenhouse-gas emissions, and livestock accounts for 14.5 percent of total global emissions, according to the United Nations. That's more than direct emissions from the transportation sector.

"In space, we don't have 10,000 or 15,000 liters of water available to produce 1 kilogram of beef," said Toubia. "This joint experiment marks a significant first step toward achieving our vision to ensure food security for generations to come while preserving our natural resources."

These efforts come as the global climate crisis and population boom continue to grow. A World Resources Institute report in July 2019 found that Americans will need to cut their average consumption of beef by about 40 percent, and Europeans by 22 percent, for the world to continue to feed the 10 billion people expected to live on this planet in 2050. In the time until then, the global demand for meat and dairy is expected to rise by nearly 70 percent. The global demand for beef, goat meat and lamb or mutton is expected to rise even more, by 88 percent.

In the face of these looming environmental dangers coupled with rising food demands, many companies are trying to find solutions. Aleph Farms has competition: Mosa Meat in the Netherlands and Memphis Meats in the US are also racing to develop in vitro or "clean" meat. Plant-based protein brands like Impossible Foods and Beyond Meat have also exploded onto the food scene in recent years. Their meatless burgers have spread to Burger King, McDonald's, Tim Hortons and even grocery stores across the US.

訳　食革命の始まり

いずれ宇宙で育った（牛肉の）ハンバーガーが食べられるようになるかもしれません。アレフ・ファームズは、牛の細胞からステーキ用牛肉を人工的に製造するイスラエルの食品企業で、国際宇宙ステーションで肉を育てることに初めて成功しました。これは屠殺（とさつ）を伴わない、環境にやさしい肉の商用生産という同社の目標に向けた大きな一歩です。

しくみは次の通り。研究者が牛から細胞を採取し、それに栄養を与え、牛の体内を模した人工的な環境に入れます。するとその細胞は培養され、結合筋組織に育ち、最終的に完全な大きさのステーキ用肉となります。アレフ・ファームズは、3Dバイオプリンティング・ソリューションズというロシアのバイオプリンティング企業と共同でこの工程を成功させました。

アレフ・ファームズによれば、この最先端の研究は、想像しうる最も極端な環境下で行われ、持続可能な食品製造法の成長可能性を示しており、その製造法によって、従来の牛肉生産に伴う土地・水の無駄遣いや汚染を避けることができるのです。

この宇宙育ちの肉は、長期にわたる有人宇宙飛行中の飛行士たちの食料を賄う一助となる可能性とともに、地球上で人口が爆発的に増えていくなかでの食料不安の対処法にもなりうると、3Dバイオプリンティング・ソリューションズは言います。アレフ・ファームズによれば、同社の製品はまだ市販できる段階にはありませんが、3、4年後には市場に並ぶ準備が整いそうだということです。

アレフ・ファームズのCEO、ディディエ・トゥビア氏がCNNに語ったところでは、工場式の畜産業は「動物とのつながりを失って」おり、屠殺を伴わないステーキ用肉の育成は「ただステーキ用肉を生み出すためのマシンにすぎないものとして」牛を用いることに代わる、より優れた選択肢だということです。

同社は、この細胞を使う工程はより人道的なだけでなく、自然環境にもよりやさしいと言います。同社の掲げる目標の1つは、環境への負荷を最小限に抑えて肉を製造することです。従来の牛肉生産は多くの土地と資源を使い尽くします。牛は、豚や家禽（かきん）より成長や生殖のペースが遅いため、はるかに多くの飼料を食べ、より多くの土地と水を必要とします。牛肉だけで家畜による温室効果ガス排出量の41％を占めており、家畜（による排出量）は世界全体の排出量の14.5％を占めると国連は発表しています。これは輸送部門からの直接的な排出量を上回る数値です。

「宇宙には、1キロの牛肉を作るのに必要な1万とか1万5000リットルの水はありません」とトゥビア氏は言います。「今回の合同実験は、来るべき世代のために食料を安定的に確保し、同時に自然資源を温存するという私たちのビジョンの達成に向けた、大きな初めの一歩なのです」

こうした取り組みは、地球の気候危機や人口爆発が拡大し続けるのを受けてのものです。世界資源研究所の2019年7月の報告で明らかにされたのは、牛肉の平均消費量をアメリカは約40％、欧州は22％削減する必要が生じるということです、2050年には100億人になると見込まれる地球人口に世界が食料を供給し続けるためには。それまでに、肉と乳製品の世界需要は70％近く増加する見通しです。牛肉、ヤギ肉、ラム肉または羊肉の世界需要はそれをさらに上回り、88％増加すると見込まれています。

食料需要の高まりとともに迫りくるこうした環境危機に直面し、多くの企業が解決策を見いだそうと努めています。アレフ・ファームズには競合相手がいます。オランダのモサ・ミートや米国のメンフィス・ミーツも、試験管肉、つまり「クリーン」ミートの開発競争でしのぎを削っています。植物由来タンパク質製品ブランドである、インポッシブルフーズやビヨンドミートもここ数年、食品業界に彗星のごとく登場してきました。肉を使わないそれらのハンバーガーは、バーガーキング、マクドナルド、ティムホートンズ、さらには米国各地の食料品店にまで広まりを見せています。

語句

engineer: ～を工学的に作り出す／cell: 細胞／
significant: 大きな、意義のある／slaughter: 屠殺／

-free: …なしの、…を用いない／nutrient: 栄養分、栄養素／artificial: 人工的な／mimic: 〜をまねる、模倣する／multiply: 増殖する／connective tissue: 結合組織／muscle tissue: 筋組織／collaborate with: 〜と協働する／bioprinting: バイオプリンティング ▶3Dプリンター医療に応用する手法。／carry out: 〜を行う、実行する／cutting-edge: 最先端の、最新の／extreme: 極端な／imaginable: 想像しうる／sustainable: 持続可能な／waste: 浪費、無駄遣い／conventional: 従来の／feed: 〜に食べ物を与える／manned space mission: 有人宇宙飛行／address: 〜に対処する／food insecurity: 食料不足、食料不安／booming: 急成長している／be commercially available: 市販されている／factory farming: 工場式農場、工場畜産場／alternative to: 〜に代わる選択肢／mere: ほんの、単なる／humane: 人道的な／minimal: 最小限の／environmental footprint: 環境フットプリント ▶製品や企業活動が環境に与える負荷を評価するための指標。／reproduce: 繁殖する、生殖する／poultry: 家禽（かきん）／be responsible for: 〜の原因である／livestock: 家畜／greenhouse-gas emissions: 温室効果ガス排出量／account for: 〜の割合を占める／the transportation sector: 輸送部門／mark: 〜を示す、〜となる／ensure: 〜を保証する、確実なものにする／food security: 食料の安全保障、食料確保／preserve: 〜を保つ、保護する／consumption: 消費／dairy:《集合的》乳製品／lamb: 子羊の肉、ラム／mutton:（成長した）羊の肉／in the face of: 〜に直面して／looming: 気味悪く迫ってくる／coupled with: 〜に加えた、〜と一緒の／competition: 競争相手、ライバル／in vitro: 試験管の中での ▶in vitro fertilization（体外受精）の形でよく使われる。／clean meat: クリーンミート ▶動物の細胞からつくる培養肉のこと。／plant-based protein: 植物由来タンパク質／explode onto the…scene: …のシーンに勢いよく登場する／Tim Hortons: ティムホートンズ ▶カナダのドーナツチェーン。

No.2

1. 正解 C

What is the news report mainly about?

(**A**) The fact that female pigs are smarter than male pigs

(**B**) A study about what pigs do for enjoyment

(**C**) The discovery that pigs use tools

設問訳 このニュースは主に何について述べているか。

(**A**) メスの豚・イノシシはオスの豚・イノシシより賢いということ

(**B**) 楽しみのために豚・イノシシは何をするかについての研究

(**C**) 豚・イノシシは道具を使うという発見

解説 第1段落の最後にwe can add tool use to the list of their accomplishments（私たちは彼らの特技のリストに「道具の使用」を加えることができる）、そして第2段落で「これまで道具を使う様子が観察されたことが一度もなかったイノシシが、口にくわえた棒で穴を掘る様子が見られた」→「これは指のない豚・イノシシが道具を使える証拠だ」と述べられている。よって、正解は（**C**）。

2. 正解 A

What was Priscilla seen doing with sticks?

(**A**) Digging

(**B**) Looking for food

(**C**) Moving mounds around

設問訳 プリシラは棒を使って何をしているところを見られたか。

(**A**) 掘るところ

(**B**) 食べ物を探すところ

(**C**) 盛り土をあちこち動かすところ

解説 第2段落のshe witnessed an adult warty pig named Priscilla digging with a stick in her mouth（彼女［＝研究論文の共著者］はプリシラという名の成長したヒゲイノシシが口にくわえた棒で穴を掘る様子を目の当たりにした）や、第3段落のshe picked up a flat piece of bark... Holding it in her mouth, she used it to dig（彼女［＝プリシラ］は平たい木の皮を拾い……それを口にくわえ、それを使って穴を掘った）という記述から、（**A**）が正解。

3. 正解 B

Why did the researchers place spatulas in the pigs' enclosure?

(**A**) To make the pigs' nests more comfortable

(**B**) To see if the pigs used them as tools

(**C**) Because the pigs couldn't move things for themselves

設問訳 研究者たちは、なぜイノシシたちの囲いの中にフライ返しを置いたのか。
(A)イノシシたちの巣をより心地よくするため
(B)イノシシたちがそれらを道具として使用するかどうかを確かめるため
(C)イノシシたちが自分たちだけで物を動かすことができなかったため

解説 第4段落で、「研究者たちが囲いの中にフライ返しを置いた」のは、The researchers wanted to see if and how Priscilla and her pen-mates would use the objects as tools.(プリシラ、そして彼女と同じ囲いにいる仲間たちが、フライ返しを道具として使うか否か、また、どのように使うのかを確認するのが目的だった)と述べられていることから、正解は(B)である。

4. 正解 C

Which of the following would Root-Bernstein probably agree with?
(A)Cognition evolves only after the development of tool use.
(B)Tool use is not a very significant development.
(C)Our usual ideas about animal intelligence need changing.

設問訳 次のうち、ルート＝バーンスタイン氏がおそらく同意するであろうことは何か。
(A)道具を使用するという進化の後でのみ認知は進化する。
(B)道具を使用するようになることは、それほど重要な進化ではない。
(C)動物の知能に関するわれわれの通常の考えを変える必要がある。

解説 最終段落でルート＝バーンスタイン氏の We might think that only humans manipulate the environment to affect their own lives, but in different ways, many other species do this too(自分たちの生活に影響を与えるために環境に手を加えるのはヒトだけだと思うかもしれないが、さまざまに異なる形で、他の多くの種も同じことをしている)という言葉が紹介されている。ここから、氏が同意するであろうことは(C)だと判断できる。

5. 正解 B

What did Root-Bernstein say her research can help us understand?
(A)How to manipulate the environment better
(B)How cognition develops
(C)What kind of species pigs evolved from

設問訳 ルート＝バーンスタイン氏によれば、彼女の研究は何に対するわれわれの理解を助けてくれるか。
(A)環境を今よりよく変える方法
(B)認知はどのように発達するのか
(C)豚・イノシシはどの種から進化したのか

解説 最終段落で、According to Root-Bernstein, ...the findings provide clues to how cognition evolves and how bodies are linked to their environments.(ルート＝バーンスタイン氏によれば……この発見は、いかに認知が進化するのか、いかに身体が自らの置かれた環境にリンクしているのかを解き明かすヒントを与えてくれる)とあることから、(B)が正解となる。

問題文 A Closer Look at Pigs

Pigs are not heralded for their intelligence, but swine are smarter than they seem. They are test subjects in studies that lead to lifesaving discoveries. They are reliable and beloved therapy animals. And now, we can add tool use to the list of their accomplishments.

According to a study in the journal *Mammalian Biology*, researchers observed a family of critically endangered Visayan warty pigs using sticks to dig and build nests—evidence that the digitless swine are capable of using tools. Pigs are not known for nest-building, and they certainly are not known for any sophisticated use of tools. They had never been observed using any before, a fact attributed to their lack of digits and their cloddish snouts. Meredith Root-Bernstein, a conservation ecologist and a co-author of the study, stumbled across the phenomenon at a Parisian zoo, where she witnessed an adult warty pig named Priscilla digging with a stick in her mouth.

"She would deposit some leaves, move them to a different spot on the mound and dig a bit with her nose," Root-Bernstein wrote in her observations. "At one point, she picked up a flat piece of bark about 10 centimeters by 40 centimeters that was lying on the mound. Holding it in her mouth, she used it to dig—lifting and pushing the soil backward—quite energetically and rapidly."

Root-Bernstein was so captivated by Priscilla that she visited the enclosure again several times, in 2015, 2016 and 2017, with a team of researchers who placed spatulas in the pigs' area. The researchers wanted to see if and how Priscilla and her penmates would use the objects as tools. However, the pigs did little with the gadgets during the researchers' first visit. Then, in 2016, Priscilla and her female offspring moved sticks in a rowing motion to dig and build a nest. Priscilla's mate Billie also dug with a stick, though his attempts were not as successful as those of her female family members, the researchers wrote.

In the 2017 trial, Priscilla dominated once again, using a stick to dig a total of seven times. But the study noted that digging with sticks in their mouths was less effective than digging with their hooves or snouts. So why, then, did the pigs do it?

Perhaps they just enjoyed it. The researchers said the pigs might view tool use as a reward that "feels good." At least, it does not appear to harm their nest-building. Or perhaps the behavior is truly beneficial to nest-building and humans have yet to figure out why. The study could not determine just why the pigs kept digging.

In any case, the behavior was likely learned among Priscilla's family. Visayan warty pigs live in family units and, like human children, study each other to learn what goes right, according to the study.

Few species have been spotted using tools to their benefit, Root-Bernstein told CNN. Primates like chimpanzees and orangutans use tools to search for food. But pigs getting handy? It was virtually unheard of in science before her observation.

"Just using tools at all is very significant," she said. "At the time, there were no scientific reports on tool use in any kind of pigs."

According to Root-Bernstein, besides being a win for pigs in the intellectual-capacity department, the findings provide clues to how cognition evolves and how bodies are linked to their environments. "We might think that only humans manipulate the environment to affect their own lives," she said, "but in different ways, many other species do this too."

訳 豚・イノシシをもっとよく見る

豚・イノシシは、その知能によって称賛の的になることはありませんが、意外に賢いのです。豚・イノシシは、人の命を救う発見につながる研究の被検体となります。また、頼れる、愛されるセラピー動物でもあります。そして今、私たちは彼らの特技のリストに「道具の使用」を加えることができるのです。

学術誌『哺乳類の生物学』に発表された研究論文によれば、研究者たちは、絶滅の危機に瀕するビサヤンヒゲイノシシのある家族が棒を使って穴を掘り、巣作りする様子を観察しました——これは、指のない豚・イノシシが道具を使えるという証拠です。豚・イノシシは巣作りをしないものと思われており、まして高度な道具の使用などないと思われています。それらが道具を使う様子が観察されたことはそれまで一度もありませんでした。これは、指の欠如と不器用な鼻によるものだと考えられてきました。保全生態学者で研究論文の共著者であるメレディス・ルート＝バーンスタイン氏は、道具を使う様子をパリの動物園で偶然、目にしました。プリシラという名の成長したヒゲイノシシが口にくわえた棒で穴を掘る様子を目の当たりにしたのです。

「彼女（プリシラ）はよく葉っぱを置いたり、それを盛り土の別の場所に移したり、鼻を使って少し穴を掘ったりしていました」とルート＝バーンスタイン氏は観察報告に記しています。「途中でプリシラは、盛り土の上にあった10センチ×40センチほどの平たい木の皮を拾いました。それを口にくわえ、それを使って穴を掘りました——土を持ち上げたり後ろに押しやったりしながら——かなり精力的に、かつ素早く」。

ルート＝バーンスタイン氏はプリシラに魅了されるあまり、2015年、2016年、2017年と複数回、研究者チームを連れて（プリシラのいる）囲いを再び訪れました。研究者たちは囲いの中にフライ返しを置きました。プリシラ、そして彼女と同じ囲いにいる仲間たちが、フライ返しを道具として使うか否か、また、どのように使うのかを確認するのが目的でした。しかし、プリシラたちは初回の調査ではそれらをほとんどいじりませんでした。そして2016年、プリシラとそのメスの子どもたちが舟をこぐような動作で棒を動かして穴を掘り、巣作りをしました。プリシラのつがいであるビリーも棒で穴を掘りましたが、彼の試みはメスの家族たちほどうまくいかなかったと、研

究者たちは記しています。

　2017年の試みで、プリシラは再び他を圧倒しました。全部で7回、棒を使って穴を掘ったのです。しかし、研究論文では、口にくわえた棒で穴を掘るのは、彼らのひづめや鼻を使った穴掘りほど効果的ではないと指摘されています。ならばなぜ、プリシラたちは棒を使って穴を掘ったのでしょうか。

　彼らはそれをただ楽しんでいたのかもしれません。研究者たちによれば、彼らは道具の使用を「気持ちのいい」褒美だと見なしている可能性があるということです。少なくとも、それは彼らの巣作りに悪影響を及ぼすものではないようです。あるいは、ひょっとすると、それは巣作りに本当に有益な行動であるのに、人間がまだその理由を解明していないだけという可能性もあります。この研究では、一体なぜプリシラたちが穴を掘り続けたのかを突き止めることはできませんでした。

　いずれにせよ、そうした行動はプリシラの家族の間で習得されたもののようです。ビサヤンヒゲイノシシは家族を構成して生活し、ヒトの子どもたちと同じように、何がうまくいくのか互いを観察しながら学ぶ、と研究論文は伝えています。

　自らの利益のために道具を使うところを見つけられた種はほとんどないとルート＝バーンスタイン氏はCNNに語りました。チンパンジーやオランウータンなどの霊長類は食料を探すために道具を使います。しかし、物を器用に使う豚・イノシシはどうでしょう？　彼女の観察以前は、科学界ではほぼ前例のないことでした。

　「道具を使うということ自体が重要なのです」と彼女は言います。「当時、いかなる種の豚・イノシシについても、道具の使用に関する科学的報告は皆無でした」。

　ルート＝バーンスタイン氏によれば、この発見は、知的領域における豚・イノシシたちの手柄であるのみならず、いかに認知が進化するのか、いかに身体が自らの置かれた環境にリンクしているのかを解き明かすヒントを与えてくれます。「自分たちの生活に影響を与えるために環境に手を加えるのはヒトだけだと思うかもしれませんが、さまざまに異なる形で、他の多くの種も同じことをしているのです」と彼女は語りました。

語句

pig: 豚　➤日本ではイノシシに分類されるものも一部含む。／herald A for B: AをBのことで称賛する／swine:《通例集合的》豚・イノシシ／test subject: 被検体／lead to:（ある結果に）つながる／lifesaving: 人の命を救う／reliable: 頼りになる、信頼できる／beloved: 愛されてい

る／accomplishment: 特技、技能／observe...doing:（観察によって）…が〜するのに気づく／critically endangered: 絶滅の危機に瀕した／Visayan warty pig: ビサヤンヒゲイノシシ／dig: 掘る／digitless:（手・足の）指のない／sophisticated: 洗練された、高度な／attribute A to B: AがBに起因すると考える、AをBの結果だと考える／digit:（手・足の）指／cloddish: 鈍重な、不器用な／snout:（豚などの）（突き出た）鼻／conservation ecologist: 保全生態学者／coauthor: 共著者／stumble across: 偶然〜に出くわす／phenomenon: 現象、事象／witness: 〜を目撃する／deposit: 〜を置く／spot: ①場所 ②《spot...doing》…が〜しているのを見つける／mound: うずたかく盛り上がった土／observation: ①《複数形》観察報告 ②観察、観測／flat: 平たい／bark: 木の皮、樹皮／soil: 土／captivate: 〜を魅了する、とりこにする／enclosure: 囲い、囲われた場所／place: 〜を置く／spatula: フライ返し／pen:（家畜の）おり、囲い／mate: ①仲間 ②（動物の）つがいの一方／gadget:（目新しい）道具、装置／offspring:（人・動物の）子／row: こぐ／motion: 動き、動作／dominate: 圧倒する／note that: 〜だと指摘する／effective: 効果的な／hoof: ひづめ　➤複数形はhoofsまたはhooves。／reward: 褒賞、褒美／be beneficial to: 〜に有益である／figure out:（よく考えた末）〜を理解する／determine: 〜を突き止める、特定する／in any case: いずれにせよ／use...to one's benefit: …を自分の利益のために使う／primate: 霊長類の動物／handy: 器用な／be unheard of: 前例がない、前代未聞である／virtually: 実質的に、ほぼ／significant: 重大な、重要な／besides: 〜に加えて／intellectual capacity: 知的能力／department: 部門、分野／findings:（研究・調査などの）結果、結論／clue to: 〜を解くための手がかり／cognition: 認知／evolve: 進化する／manipulate: 〜を操作する、〜に手を加える／affect: 〜に影響を及ぼす

© Public domain

解答欄にご自身の解答を書き写しておくと、スコアが出しやすくなります。

Listening Section リスニング編

Part	No.	Question	解答欄	正解	測定する力
1	1	1		treatments	書き取り
		2		outbreak	書き取り
	2	1		debt	書き取り
		2		approaching	書き取り
2	1	1		B	大意把握
		2		A	詳細理解
	2	1		C	大意把握
		2		B	詳細理解
	3	1		B	大意把握
		2		C	詳細理解
3	1	1		C	大意把握
		2		C	詳細理解
		3		A	詳細理解
		4		B	話者の意図推測
		5		B	詳細理解
	2	1		B	大意把握
		2		A	詳細理解
		3		A	詳細理解
		4		C	詳細理解
		5		C	話者の意図推測
4	1	1		B	大意把握
		2		C	詳細理解
		3		B	詳細理解
		4		C	話者の意図推測
		5		A	詳細理解
	2	1		B	大意把握
		2		C	詳細理解
		3		C	話者の意図推測
		4		A	詳細理解
		5		B	詳細理解

Reading Section リーディング編

Part	No.	Question	解答欄	正解	測定する力
1	1	——		**A**	語彙
	2	——		**B**	語彙
	3	——		**A**	語彙
	4	——		**C**	語彙
2	1	1		**B**	大意把握
		2		**A**	詳細理解
	2	1		**A**	大意把握
		2		**C**	詳細理解
	3	1		**A**	大意把握
		2		**B**	詳細理解
3	1	1		**A**	大意把握
		2		**B**	詳細理解
		3		**A**	詳細理解
		4		**B**	詳細理解
		5		**A**	話者の意図推測
	2	1		**A**	大意把握
		2		**A**	詳細理解
		3		**C**	話者の意図推測
		4		**B**	詳細理解
		5		**C**	詳細理解

スコア （配点は各2点です）	リスニング（30問） 　　　　　　／60	リーディング（20問） 　　　　　　／40	合計 　　　　　　／100

上の表から、それぞれの「測定する力」の正解数を数え、下の欄に記入しましょう。
あなたの強みと弱点が一目でわかります。

リスニング	書き取り　／4	大意把握　／7	詳細理解　／15	話者の意図推測　／4
リーディング	語彙　／4	大意把握　／5	詳細理解　／9	話者の意図推測　／2

TEST 2

Listening Section リスニング編

Part 1 ディクテーション問題

Well, there's optimism about two new ①__treatments__ for Ebola. They're proving so effective they're being offered to all patients in the Democratic Republic of Congo, where the current ②__outbreak__ is the second-deadliest ever. Eighteen hundred people have died since last summer.

訳

さて、エボラ出血熱の2種類の新たな治療薬について楽観的な見方が出ています。それらは非常に有効であることが判明しつつあるため、コンゴ民主共和国のすべての患者に提供されます。同国における現在のエボラ出血熱の流行は、死者数が史上2番目の規模となっています。昨年の夏以降、1800人が亡くなっています。

語句

optimism: 楽観、楽観的見方 / treatment: 治療、治療薬 / prove（to be）: 〜だとわかる、判明する / effective: 有効な、効果的な / patient: 患者 / current: 現在の / outbreak:（病気の）流行 / deadly: 致死の、命取りの

New figures released Wednesday by the Institute of International Finance show combined US public- and private-sector ①__debt__ was close to $70 trillion. In just simple terms of dollars and cents, America's national ①__debt__ hits a new record high every second, ②__approaching__ $23 trillion right now, about $68,000 for every man, woman and child.

訳

国際金融協会が水曜日に公表した新たな統計によると、米国の公的部門・民間部門を合わせた債務が70兆ドル近くになったということです。ごく簡単に金額で言うと、アメリカの政府債務は1秒ごとに史上最高値を更新しており、現在23兆ドル、つまり男性、女性、子ども1人当たりおよそ6万8000ドルに迫っています。

語句

figure: 数字、統計 / release: 〜を公表する / the Institute of International Finance: 国際金融協会 / combined A and B: AとBを合わせた / public sector: 公的部門 / private sector: 民間部門 / debt: 債務、負債 / trillion: 1兆 / in terms of: 〜の観点から言うと / dollars and cents: 金銭 / hit a record high: 過去最高を記録する / every second: 毎秒、刻一刻と / approach: 〜に近づく

Part 2 ショートニュース問題

1. 正解 B

What is the main point of the news report?

(A) Humans have altered the land to make it more suitable for animals.

(B) Humans are to blame for a number of environmental problems.

(C) Humans are responsible for the recent decrease in ocean pollution.

設問訳 このニュースの主旨は何か。

(**A**) 人間は、動物により適した環境にするために陸地を変えた。

(**B**) いくつかの環境問題の責任は人間にある。

(**C**) 近年の海洋汚染の減少は人間のおかげである。

語句　suitable for: 〜に適した／a number of: いくつかの／be responsible for: 〜に対する功績がある

解説 ニュースの主旨（main point）を問う問題。ニュース前半で「現在地球が直面している社会的・生態学的緊急事態の責任は人類にある」と述べ、後半で「種の絶滅の危機」「陸地の変貌」「海洋プラスチック汚染」は it is all the fault of the human population（そのすべてが人類の責任だ）とあるので、これを言い換えた（**B**）が正解となる。

---

2. 正解 A

What does the news report say has happened since 1980?

(**A**) Ocean plastic pollution has increased 10 times.

(**B**) Around 1 million species of animals have become extinct.

(**C**) Around 75 percent of all land has been altered.

設問訳 このニュースによると、1980年以降何が起こっているか。

(**A**) 海洋プラスチック汚染が10倍悪化している。

(**B**) 約100万種の動物が絶滅した。

(**C**) 陸地全体のおよそ75％が変えられた。

解説 around 1 million species are in danger of becoming extinct（約100万種が絶滅の危機にある）とは言っているが、「絶滅した」とは言っていないので（**B**）はまちがい。また、（**C**）は in just the past 50 years（このわずか50年の間）に起こったことで、設問の1980年以降の問題としてあてはまるのは（**A**）だけとなる。

問題文　Damning Report on Earth Crisis

And now to a disturbing study on the fate of our planet. In just the last hour, a UN-backed environmental report was released, highlighting the social and ecological emergency the earth now faces, and we are to blame. Research shows that around 1 million species are in danger of becoming extinct—1 million—and in just the past 50 years, 75 percent of all land has been significantly altered.

Meanwhile, plastic pollution in the world's oceans has become 10 times worse since 1980. And it is all the fault of the human population.

訳　地球の危機に関する厳しい報告書

さて次は、地球の運命に関する懸念すべき研究についてです。つい先ほど、国連の支援を受けた環境報告書が公表されましたが、その報告書は、現在地球が直面している社会的・生態学的緊急事態を浮き彫りにし、その責任は私たち人類にあるとしています。研究によると、約100万種が絶滅の危機にあり——100万です——このわずか50年の間に、陸地全体の75％が大きく変えられたということです。同時に、世界の海のプラスチック汚染は1980年以来、10倍悪化しています。そのすべてが人類の責任なのです。

語句

damning: 非常に批判的な／disturbing: 心配させる、不安にさせる／fate: 運命／our planet: 地球／in just the last hour: つい先ほど／UN-backed: 国連の支援を受けた／highlight: 〜を強調する、浮き彫りにする／ecological: 生態学的な／emergency: 緊急事態／face:（問題などに）直面する／be to blame:（失敗や過失などに対する）責任がある／species:（生物の）種／be in danger of doing: 〜する危機に瀕している／become extinct: 絶滅する／significantly: 大いに／alter: 〜を変える／meanwhile: それと同時に、その一方で／plastic pollution: プラスチック汚染／fault:（誤り・落ち度の）責任、原因

1. 正解 C

What is the news report mainly about?
(**A**) Global banking
(**B**) Improvements in education
(**C**) Gender equality

設問訳 このニュースは主に何について述べているか。
(**A**) 国際銀行業務
(**B**) 教育の改善
(**C**) 男女平等

解説 冒頭の The world is moving towards legal gender equality but very, very, slowly. を聞き逃さないようにしよう。Researchers measured eight indicators of women's equality（研究者たちは、女性が獲得している平等を8つの指標で測り）や、the organization started measuring equality between the genders（同組織がジェンダー間の平等を算出し始めた）という内容から、このニュースは「男女平等」に関するものだとわかる。よって、正解は（**C**）。

2. 正解 B

Which country was found to be the least gender-equal?
(**A**) The Democratic Republic of the Congo
(**B**) Saudi Arabia
(**C**) The United States

設問訳 男女平等が最も遅れているとわかったのはどの国か。
(**A**) コンゴ民主共和国
(**B**) サウジアラビア
(**C**) アメリカ合衆国

解説 世界銀行が発表した男女平等に関する調査で、スコアが最も低かった国を答える問いである。while Saudi Arabia's overall score was the worst in the world から、「サウジアラビアの総合得点が世界で最も低かった」ことがわかる。よって、正解は（**B**）。

問題文 International Study Shows Slow Progress

The world is moving towards legal gender equality but very, very, slowly. This is according to a new report from the World Bank. Researchers measured eight indicators of women's equality and found only six countries, including Belgium, Denmark and France, scored full marks out of 100. That's an increase from none a decade ago, when the organization started measuring equality between the genders. The United States' score didn't even finish in the global top 50, while Saudi Arabia's overall score was the worst in the world. The country that improved the most was the Democratic Republic of Congo, scoring a 42 a decade ago and 70 in this report. Overall, the global average shows women receive just three-quarters of the legal rights that men do.

訳 国際調査が示す遅い進展

世界は法的な男女平等に向けて進んでいます。しかし、とても、とてもゆっくりとです。これは、世界銀行が発表した新たな調査報告書によるものです。研究者たちは、女性が獲得している平等を8つの指標で測り、ベルギー、デンマーク、フランスなどの6カ国のみが100点満点に該当するとの結論に至りました。同組織がジェンダー間の平等を算出し始めた10年前の（該当国）ゼロからは増加しています。米国のスコアは世界トップ50にすら届かず、サウジアラビアの総合得点は世界で最も低い結果となりました。最も改善が見られたのはコンゴ民主共和国で、10年前の42点に対して、今回の報告書では70点を獲得しています。全体的に見て、世界平均が示しているのは、女性が享受している法的権利は男性のわずか4分の3にすぎないということです。

語句

legal: 法的な／measure: 〜を測定する／indicator: 指標／the Democratic Republic of Congo: ➤ Congo の前に the を付けるのが正式。

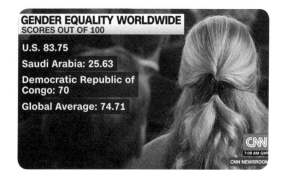

GENDER EQUALITY WORLDWIDE
SCORES OUT OF 100
U.S. 83.75
Saudi Arabia: 25.63
Democratic Republic of Congo: 70
Global Average: 74.71
CNN
7:09 AM GMT
CNN NEWSROOM

1. 正解 B

What is the main point of the news report?

(**A**) The measles virus is no longer a threat in developed countries.

(**B**) The incidence of measles is on the rise around the world.

(**C**) The measles virus has been eliminated in the US.

設問訳 このニュースの主旨は何か。

(**A**) はしかウイルスは、先進諸国ではもはや脅威ではない。

(**B**) はしかの発症率が世界中で上昇している。

(**C**) はしかウイルスは、米国では撲滅されている。

語句 threat: 脅威／incidence:（病気などの）発症率

解説 冒頭のis making a global resurgence の意味がわからなくても、続くIn the US, the virus was declared eliminated in the year 2000. But this year, the number of cases has skyrocketed... で、(**A**)(**C**) は事実と異なると判断できる。その後、Globally で始まる1文でcases are three times higher... と述べられているので、正解は(**B**)。

2. 正解 C

What happened in the US in the year 2000?

(**A**) The number of measles cases skyrocketed.

(**B**) There were three times more measles cases than in 2018.

(**C**) Measles was declared to have been eliminated.

設問訳 米国では2000年に何が起こったか。

(**A**) はしかの感染者数が急増した。

(**B**) 2018年と比べてはしかの感染者が3倍多かった。

(**C**) はしかの撲滅が宣言された。

解説 In the US, the virus was declared eliminated in the year 2000. のwas declared eliminated（撲滅されたと宣言された）の部分が聞き取れれば、(**C**) が正解とわかる。the virus（ウイルス）は、冒頭のmeasles（はしか）のウイルスのこと。(**A**) も (**B**) も2000年ではなく、このニュースが放送された年（2019年）の出来事である。

問題文　Old Foe Returns

Well, measles, once nearly eradicated in the developed world, is making a global resurgence. In the US, the virus was declared eliminated in the year 2000. But this year, the number of cases has skyrocketed, with over 700 people infected in 22 states. Well, that's according to the Centers for Disease Control. Globally, according to the World Health Organization, cases are three times higher the first four months of the year, compared to the same period in 2018. This highly contagious disease continues to sicken and even kill children and vulnerable people, especially in countries with poor vaccination rates.

訳　宿敵の復活

さて、はしかは、先進諸国では一度ほぼ根絶されましたが、世界的に再流行しています。米国では、はしかウイルスの撲滅が2000年に宣言されました。しかし今年、感染者数が急増し、22州で700人以上が感染しています。これは米疾病対策センターの発表によるものです。世界的にも、こちらは世界保健機関によるものですが、今年初めの4カ月の感染者数が2018年の同時期と比べて3倍多くなっています。この感染力の強い病気は、いまだに子どもたちや病気にかかりやすい人たちに感染し、死に至らしめることもあります。とりわけワクチン接種率の低い国々でそうなっています。

語句

old foe: 宿敵／measles: はしか／eradicate: 〜を撲滅する、根絶する／make a resurgence: 復活する／virus: ウイルス／declare A B: AをBだと宣言する／eliminated: 排除された、取り除かれた／case: 患者、症例／skyrocket: 急上昇する／infected: 感染した／the Centers for Disease Control (and Prevention):

米疾病対策センター／the World Health Organization: 世界保健機関／compared to: ～と比べて／highly contagious: 伝染性の高い、感染力の強い／

disease: 病気／continue to do: ～し続ける／sicken: ～を病気にさせる／vulnerable: 脆弱な、病気にかかりやすい／vaccination rate: ワクチン接種率

Part 3 ニュース問題

No.1

問題文 ③⑨↓ 設問 ④⓪↓

アメリカ英語

1. 正解 C

What is the main issue discussed in the news report?

(A) A GoFundMe page for a California teacher
(B) Increasing cases of cancer among public-school teachers
(C) Sick-leave policy for California teachers

設問訳 このニュースで論じられている主な問題は何か。

(A) カリフォルニア州のある教師のための「GoFundMe」のページ
(B) 公立学校の教師の間でがん患者が増えていること
(C) カリフォルニア州の教師のための病気休暇政策

解説 冒頭で「サンフランシスコの小学校教師が乳がんを患い、休職期間を延長しているが、代理教員の給与を自腹で支払わなければならない」と問題提起し、It's all part of a little-known state policy that dates back decades.（これはもっぱら数十年前からある、ほとんど知られていない州の政策の一部によるもの）と述べている。その後、この「教員のための病気休暇（sick leave）に関する州の政策（state policy）」の具体的な説明が続く。よって、ニュースが取り上げている問題は（C）だとわかる。

2. 正解 C

What did the sick teacher have to pay for?

(A) 100 days of sick leave
(B) Disability insurance under a state program
(C) A substitute to teach her classes

設問訳 この病気を患っている教師は、何のために支払いをしなければならなかったか。

(A) 100日間の病気休暇
(B) 州のプログラムに基づく障害保険
(C) 彼女の代わりに授業をする代理教員

解説 このニュースで言及されている教師が、「何のために支払いをしなければならなかったのか」については冒頭で述べられている。she's having to pay money out of her own pocket for a substitute teacher（彼女は、代理教員の給与を自腹で支払わなければならない）ということから、正解は（C）となる。

3. 正解 A

What is true about public-school teachers in California?

(A) They must pay for substitutes to teach their classes if they take extended leave.
(B) Teachers with serious illnesses are not allowed to take extended sick leave.
(C) Disability insurance pays their salaries when they are on sick leave.

設問訳 カリフォルニア州の公立学校教員について正しい記述は何か。

(A) 休職期間を延長する場合は、代わりに授業を受け持つ代理教員の給与を支払わなければならない。
(B) 重い病気にかかっている教員は、病気休暇の延長を認められない。
(C) 病気休暇中は、障害保険から彼らの給与が支払われる。

解説 ニュースの序盤で、カリフォルニア州の制度に関する説明がある。California teachers get 10 sick days a year. If they need more, they can take an additional 100 days of extended sick leave.（カリフォルニア州の教員は病気休暇を年間10日取得できる。さらなる必要が生じれば、病気休暇を延長して追加で100日取得することが可能）とあるので、「休暇の延長は認められない」とする（B）は不適。その直後に、But there's a catch: the teachers have to pay for their own subs.（しかし、落とし穴がある。同州の教員は、自分の代行を務める教師の給与を負担しなければならないのだ）とあるので、正解は（A）。

4. 正解 B

What can be inferred from the statement by the San Francisco teachers union?

(**A**) The union is asking schools to hire more substitute teachers.

(**B**) The union will address the sick-leave problem through contract negotiations.

(**C**) The number of sick days that teachers can take cannot be increased.

設問訳 サンフランシスコの教職員組合による声明から推測できることは何か。

(**A**) 組合は学校にもっと代理教員を雇用するよう求めている。

(**B**) 組合は契約交渉を通して病気休暇の問題に対処する。

(**C**) 教員が取得できる病気休暇の日数は増やすことができない。

解説 カリフォルニア州では、教員は病気休暇を年間10日取得できるが、病気休暇を延長する場合は代理教員の給料を自腹で支払わなくてはならない。ニュースの中盤で、この問題についてサンフランシスコの教職員組合が出した声明の内容が述べられている。it's "consulting with our members on their priorities...making improvements in this and other parts of the contract." の部分から、(**B**) が推測できると言える。

5. 正解 B

What have some educators said is to blame for the situation in California?

(**A**) The increasing number of teachers with serious illnesses

(**B**) A lack of funding for public education

(**C**) The rising cost of hiring substitute teachers

設問訳 一部の教育関係者は、カリフォルニア州のこの状況を引き起こした原因は何だと言っているか。

(**A**) 重い病気にかかっている教員数の増加

(**B**) 公教育の資金不足

(**C**) 代理教員の雇用費の上昇

解説 この問題の諸悪の根源について、Educators say it's part of a larger issue about the lack of money in public education.（教育関係者によると、これは公教育の資金不足をめぐる、より大きな問題の一部だというこ

とだ）と述べられている。（**B**）のfundingとはmoneyのことなので、（**B**）が最適。このすぐ後の "We need to fix funding..."で、さらに詳しい現状が補足説明されている。

問題文 **Heavy Burden for Sick Teachers**

She's a popular second-grade teacher at San Francisco's Glen Park Elementary, and she has breast cancer. Now on extended leave, she's having to pay money out of her own pocket for a substitute teacher.

It's all part of a little-known state policy that dates back decades. Here's how it works. California teachers get 10 sick days a year. If they need more, they can take an additional 100 days of extended sick leave. But there's a catch: the teachers have to pay for their own subs. The money gets docked from their paychecks, about $200 per day in the case of the San Francisco teacher, who wishes to remain anonymous.

It falls under a 1976 provision in which teachers don't pay into the state's disability-insurance program, so they don't get those benefits. In a statement, the San Francisco teachers union says it's "consulting with our members on their priorities for contract negotiations next year. As always, we look forward to making improvements in this and other parts of the contract."

Educators say it's part of a larger issue about the lack of money in public education.

"We need to fix funding in California. We're the fifth-largest economy in the world, and we pay 42nd in rankings per state in what we spend per pupil on education. That's just not right."（Eric Heins, California Teachers Association）

It's not clear how many times this has happened, but it was a GoFundMe page that brought the issue to light, the teacher being fully reimbursed and beyond.

It's going to take California lawmakers and the teachers unions to come up with a fix for what everyone seems to acknowledge is ridiculous: a cancer-ridden teacher, with all the stresses and worries associated with an illness, having to pay for her own substitute.

Dan Simon, CNN, San Francisco.

訳　病気の教師にとって重い負担

彼女は、サンフランシスコのグレンパーク小学校の2年生を受け持つ人気教師で、乳がんを患っています。現在、休職期間を延長中の彼女は、代理教員の給与を自腹で支払わなければなりません。

これはもっぱら数十年前からある、ほとんど知られていない州の政策の一部によるものです。そのしくみはこうです。カリフォルニア州の教員は病気休暇を年間10日取得できます。さらなる必要が生じれば、病気休暇を延長して追加で100日取得することが可能です。しかし、落とし穴があります。同州の教員は、自分の代行を務める教師の給与を負担しなければならないのです。その金は彼らの給与から天引きされ、匿名を望むこのサンフランシスコの教師の場合、1日当たり約200ドルになります。

これは1976年に定められた（カリフォルニア州法の）ある規定に該当するもので、教員は州の障害保険プログラムに加入しない、したがって彼らはその給付を受けない、とされています。声明の中で、サンフランシスコの教職員組合は、「組合員たちと来年度の（雇用）契約交渉の優先事項について協議している。いつも通り、われわれはこの項目だけではなく、契約のいくつかの項目の改善を期待する」と述べています。

教育関係者によると、これは公教育の資金不足をめぐる、より大きな問題の一部だということです。

「カリフォルニア州の資金問題を解決する必要があります。カリフォルニア州は世界第5位の経済規模を有しているにもかかわらず、教育において児童・生徒1人当たりに費やす金額では、州ごとのランキングで（50州中）42位なのです。これはどう考えても間違っています」（エリック・ハインズ　カリフォルニア州教職員協会）

この規定に当たる事例がこれまでに何件生じているのか明らかではありませんが、この問題を白日の下にさらしたのは「GoFundMe」のページで、件の教師には（代理教員の給与に支払った）全額分を上回る額の寄付が寄せられました。

カリフォルニア州議会と教職員組合は解決策を打ち出す必要があるでしょう、ばかげていると誰もが認識していると思われるこの事態、つまり、がんに苦しむ教師が、その病気からくるストレスや心配事を抱えながら、自分の代理教員の給与を負担しなければならないという事態に対して。

CNNのダン・サイモンがサンフランシスコからお伝えしました。

語句

heavy burden: 重い負担／second-grade: 2年生の／breast cancer: 乳がん／(be) on leave: 休暇・休職中である／extended: 延長された／out of one's own pocket: 自腹を切って／substitute: ①代理の ②代理教員／date back: （年月を）さかのぼる／additional: 追加の／sick leave: 病気休暇／catch: わな、落とし穴／sub: ＝substitute teacher／dock A from B: AをBから差し引く／paycheck: 給料、給与／anonymous: 匿名の／fall under: 〜に該当する／provision:（法律などの）条項／disability insurance: 身体障害保険／benefits: 給付金／statement: 声明／consult with: 〜と協議する、相談する／priority: 優先事項／contract negotiation: 契約交渉／make an improvement: 改善する／fix: ①〜を改善する、直す ②解決策／funding: 資金提供、資金調達／pupil: 児童、生徒／GoFundMe: ▶米国のクラウドファンディングのプラットフォーム。／bring...to light: …を明るみに出す／reimburse: 〜に（経費などを）弁済する／lawmaker: 立法者、議員／ridiculous: ばかげた、とんでもない／-ridden:《通例複合語で》…に悩まされた、苦しめられた／with all: 〜がありながら、〜にもかかわらず／(be) associated with: 〜に関係する、付随する

No.2　問題文 41↓ 設問 42↓　イギリス英語

1.　正解　B

What problem in the UK is the main topic of the news report?

(**A**) Children having to deliver food to earn money

(**B**) Worsening lack of food among the poor

(**C**) Breaches of policy by human-rights campaigners

設問訳 英国のどのような問題がこのニュースの主題となっているか。

(A) 金を稼ぐために食料を配達しなければならない子どもたち

(B) 貧困者の間での食料不足の悪化

(C) 人権活動家による政策の不履行

解説 poverty（貧困）、go hungry（飢える）、without food（食料なしで）、emergency food parcels（緊急食料パック）、food aid（食料援助）、food bank（フードバンク）などのキーワードから、英国における貧困、特に食料不足の問題を取り上げたニュースであることをつかみたい。ニュース序盤で、Billy McGranaghan has been delivering...The situation, he says, is getting worse. と述べられ、後半でも the rising levels of food poverty と述べられていることから、(B) が正解としてふさわしい。

2. 正解 A

What criticism has been made of the UK government?

(A) That it has not made sure that citizens have enough food

(B) That it has prevented charities from helping hungry families

(C) That its policies have forced many food banks to close

設問訳 どんな批判が英国政府に対してなされているか。

(A) 市民が十分な食料を確実に得られるようにしていない

(B) 慈善団体がおなかをすかせた家族を助けるのを妨げた

(C) 政府の政策によって、多くのフードバンクが閉鎖を余儀なくされた

語句 make sure that: 確実に〜するようにする／prevent...from doing: …が〜するのを妨げる／force...to do: …が〜するのを余儀なくさせる

解説 前半に出てくる Campaigners argue it's a breach of the UK government's human-rights obligations to ensure adequate food. が該当箇所。よって、正解は (A)。

3. 正解 A

Who has been supplying food aid to needy citizens in the UK?

(A) Charities

(B) Campaigners

(C) Policymakers

設問訳 英国の困窮している市民に食料援助を提供しているのは誰か。

(A) 慈善団体

(B) 活動家

(C) 政策立案者

解説 中盤で In just the past five years, the country's largest food-bank charity... It's now delivering nearly 1.6 million emergency food parcels a year.（わずかこの5年で、英国最大のフードバンク団体は……現在、年間160万個近くもの緊急食料パックを配達している）と述べられていることから、正解は (A) となる。Is it appropriate for government to stand by as families go hungry, and just wait for charities to step in and fill the gap?（おなかをすかせている家族がいるのに政府がそれを傍観し、慈善団体が介入してその穴を埋めるのをただ待っているというのは適切なことなのか）という男性のコメントにも charities が使われている。

4. 正解 C

What did the report by Human Rights Watch say about single mothers?

(A) They deliver food parcels to make money.

(B) They send their children to food banks to ask for food.

(C) They sometimes miss meals in order to feed their children.

設問訳 ヒューマン・ライツ・ウォッチの報告書は、シングルマザーについてどう述べていたか。

(A) 彼女たちはお金を稼ぐために食料パックを配達している。

(B) 彼女たちは子どもたちにフードバンクへ食料をもらいに行かせている。

(C) 彼女たちは子どもたちに食べさせるために、食事を抜くことがある。

解説 シングルマザーに関するヒューマン・ライツ・ウォッチの報告について、It gives several examples of single mothers skipping meals so that their children have something to eat.（報告書には、子どもたちに何か食べさせるために自分の食事を抜いているシングルマザーの例が数件挙げられている）と述べられていることから、

（**C**）が正解とわかる。

5. 正解 **C**

What does the statement by the government spokesperson imply?

（**A**）The government has sent needy children to live in wealthy households.

（**B**）The government is giving working families money to relocate.

（**C**）The criticism against the government does not reflect reality.

設問訳 政府の報道官の声明が暗に示していることは何か。

（**A**）政府は貧しい子どもたちを裕福な家庭で暮らせるようにしてきた。

（**B**）政府は勤労世帯に引っ越し資金を給付している。

（**C**）政府に対する批判は現実を反映していない。

解説 十分な食料が人々に行き渡っていないのは政府による緊縮措置のせいだというヒューマン・ライツ・ウォッチの報告に対して、In a statement, a UK government spokesperson has dismissed the latest criticism, describing the report as misleading.（ある声明で、英国政府の報道官は、その報告書は誤解を招くものだとして、最近の批判をはねつけている）とあり、「英国政府への批判は事実とは異なる」という報道官の考えがわかる。よって、正解は（**C**）。

問題文 More Help Needed for the Needy

Driving through affluent West London, the poverty isn't immediately obvious. Billy McGranaghan has been delivering food aid in this part of London for years. The situation, he says, is getting worse.

"When you actually see the poverty of the…with children not havin' enough, it does get to you."（Billy McGranaghan, founder of Dad's House Charity）

Campaigners argue it's a breach of the UK government's human-rights obligations to ensure adequate food.

"The United Kingdom is a country with the fifth-largest economy in the world. It really beggars belief that, in this country, increasing numbers, year on year, of…of families are going hungry, without food."（Kartik Raj, Human Rights Watch）

In just the past five years, the country's largest food-bank charity has recorded an increase of close to 50 percent. It's now delivering nearly 1.6 million emergency food parcels a year.

"In addition to being a legal question, it's also a simple moral question: Is it appropriate for a government to stand by as families go hungry, and just wait for charities to step in and fill the gap?"（Kartik Raj）

The Human Rights Watch report is damning. It gives several examples of single mothers skipping meals so that their children have something to eat.

The charity directly links the rising levels of food poverty to the UK government's austerity drive over the past decade, an issue that's proved a flash point in British politics.

In a statement, a UK government spokesperson has dismissed the latest criticism, describing the report as misleading.

"We're helping parents to move into work to give families the best opportunity to move out of poverty. And it's working—employment is at a record high, and children growing up in working households are five times less likely to be in relative poverty."（Statement by spokesperson for the UK Department for Work and Pensions）

For those relying on food aid now, the government's words are of little comfort.

"A lot of families can't…can't afford electricity. They can't afford to cook when they do get the food banks."（Billy McGranaghan）

A situation, he says, that's unlikely to change anytime soon.

Bianca Nobilo, CNN, London.

訳 困窮者に必要なさらなる援助

富裕層が暮らすロンドン西部を車で通り抜けていても、そこにある貧困はすぐには見えてきません。ビリー・マグラナガンさんは数年前からロンドンのこの地区で支援食料の配達を続けています。状況は悪化している、と彼は言います。

「その貧困状態……十分におなかが満たされない子どもたちを実際に目の当たりにすると、本当に胸が痛くなりますよ」（ビリー・マグラナガン　慈善団体ダッズハウス創設者）

活動家たちの主張によれば、これは英国政府による、十分な食料を保証するという人権に関する義務の不履行です。

「英国は世界で第5位の経済大国です。本当に信じがたいことです、この国で、食べ物がなく、おなかをすかせている家族が年々増えているなんて」(カーティック・ラジ ヒューマン・ライツ・ウォッチ)

わずかこの5年で、英国最大のフードバンク団体は50%近くの利用増加を記録しています。同団体は現在、年間160万個近くもの緊急食料パックを配達しているのです。

「法的な問題であるのに加え、単純に倫理的な問題でもあります。おなかをすかせている家族がいるのに政府がそれを傍観し、慈善団体が介入してその穴を埋めるのをただ待っているというのは適切なことなのか、というね」(カーティック・ラジ)

ヒューマン・ライツ・ウォッチの報告は非常に批判的です。報告書には、子どもたちに何か食べさせるために自分の食事を抜いているシングルマザーの例が数件挙げられています。

この慈善団体は、食料貧困率の上昇は過去10年にわたる英国政府の緊縮措置に直接の原因があるとみています。緊縮措置は英国政治において激しく議論される問題となっています。

ある声明で、英国政府の報道官は、その報告書は誤解を招くものだとして、最近の批判をはねつけています。

「われわれ政府は、貧困から抜け出す最高の機会を家族に与えるために親たちが仕事に就けるよう支援しています。そして、それはうまく機能しています。雇用水準は記録的な高さで、勤労世帯で育つ子どもたちは(以前より)5倍も相対的貧困に陥りにくくなっているのです」(英雇用年金局報道官の声明)

現在、食料援助に頼っている人たちにとって、こうした政府の言葉はほとんど何の慰めにもなりません。

「多くの家庭では電気代が支払えないのです。仮にフードバンク(から食料)を入手できたとしても、それを調理することができないのです」(ビリー・マグラナガン)

彼が言うには、状況はしばらく改善しそうにないということです。

CNNのビアンカ・ノビロがロンドンからお伝えしました。

語句

the needy:《集合的》貧困者たち、困窮者たち/affluent: 裕福な、富裕な/poverty: 貧困/deliver: ～を配達する/food aid: 食料援助、食料支援/get to:

～の胸を痛ませる/campaigner: 運動家、活動家/argue (that): ～であると主張する/breach: 違反、不履行/human-rights obligation: 人権に関する義務/ensure: ～を保証する/adequate: 十分な、適切な/it beggars belief that: ～というのは信じがたい/year on year: 年々/Human Rights Watch: ヒューマン・ライツ・ウォッチ ▶米国に本拠地を持つ国際人権NGO。/charity: 慈善事業、慈善団体/record: ①～を記録する②記録的な/close to: ～近くの/emergency: 緊急の/parcel: 小包、小荷物/in addition to: ～に加えて/legal: 法的な/moral: 道徳的な、倫理的な/appropriate: 適切な/stand by: 傍観する/go hungry: 飢えている、空腹でいる/step in: 介入する/fill a gap: 不足を補う、空白を埋める/damning:〈報告などが〉非常に批判的な/skip a meal: 食事を抜く/link A to B: AをBに結びつけて考える/austerity drive: 一連の緊縮措置/prove (to be): ～であることがわかる/flash point: 議論の引火点、論争を招く話題/statement: 声明/dismiss: ～を退ける、軽く片付ける/criticism: 批判、非難/describe A as B: AをBだと言う/misleading: 誤解を招くような/move into: (新しい仕事などを)始める/work: ①仕事、職 ②機能する、うまくいく/move out of poverty: 貧困から抜け出す/employment: 雇用、雇用率/working household: 勤労世帯/be likely to do: ～しそうである、～する可能性が高い/relative poverty: 相対的貧困/UK Department for Work and Pensions: 英雇用年金局/rely on: ～に頼る、～を当てにする/comfort: 慰め/can't afford: ①～を支払う余裕がない ②《can't afford to do》～する金銭的余裕がない/anytime soon: 近いうちに、近い将来

Part 4 インタビュー問題

No.1

問題文 (44) 設問 (45)

アメリカ英語(Fareed Zakaria)／**イギリス英語**(Jane Goodall)

1. 正解 B

What aspect of Jane Goodall's life is the interview mainly about?

(**A**) Her travels in Africa

(**B**) Her research on chimpanzees

(**C**) Her family relationships

設問訳 このインタビューは、ジェーン・グドール氏の人生のどのような面が主題になっているか。

(**A**) 彼女のアフリカ旅行

(**B**) 彼女のチンパンジー研究

(**C**) 彼女の家族関係

解説 冒頭でインタビュアーがグドール氏のキャリアについて述べていることに注意。Jane Goodall began her work that changed how we all think about animals. (ジェーン・グドール氏は皆の動物への認識を改めさせることになった仕事を開始した)、さらに She traveled to Tanzania and ended up living among the species which is the closest relative to us humans. (彼女はタンザニアへ赴き、やがて、われわれ人間に最も近い種と共に暮らすようになった) と紹介している。冒頭では触れられていないが、その後に続くグドール氏の答えには何度も chimpanzee(s) が出てくることから、正解は (**B**) だとわかる。the species which is the closest relative to us humans は当然 chimpanzees のこと。

2. 正解 C

What did Goodall learn from her mother that she passes on to others?

(**A**) You should try to bring opportunities to deprived communities.

(**B**) Even boring jobs can be opportunities.

(**C**) You should work very hard and never give up.

設問訳 グドール氏が人々に伝えている母からの教えとは何か。

(**A**) 貧困地域に機会をもたらすよう努めるべきである。

(**B**) つまらない仕事でさえもチャンスになり得る。

(**C**) 精いっぱい努力し、決して諦めないようにすべきである。

解説 my mother, my amazing mother, said... で始まるグドール氏の発言に答えがある。extremely でより意味を強調した work hard (努力をする) と、否定文で使われている give up (諦める) から、その教えとは「並々ならぬ努力をし、諦めてはいけない」ということだとわかる。これに適合するのは (**C**)。

3. 正解 B

What led to the extension of funding for Goodall's research?

(**A**) Her visit to the National Geographic Society

(**B**) Her discovery of a chimpanzee that used tools

(**C**) Her discovery of a rare, white ape

設問訳 グドール氏の研究への資金提供が継続されるきっかけになったこととは何か。

(**A**) 彼女がナショナル・ジオグラフィック協会を訪れたこと

(**B**) 彼女が道具を使うチンパンジーを発見したこと

(**C**) 彼女が珍しい白いサルを発見したこと

解説 グドール氏の発言に And it was that that enabled Leakey to go to [the] National Geographic Society. Not only did they agree to continue to fund the research,... とある。1つ目の that が指す内容は、直前の And one chimpanzee, darling David Greybeard—he's the one I saw using and making tools... なので、これを短く言い換えた (**B**) が正解となる。

4. 正解 C

What does Goodall imply about dealing with chimpanzees?

(**A**) Showing them how to use tools increases their trust.

(**B**) If they don't come to trust you quickly, they never will.

(**C**) Variety and change make them cautious.

設問訳 グドール氏がチンパンジーとの付き合いについて暗に述べていることは何か。

(**A**) 道具の使い方を見せると彼らの信頼が増す。

(**B**) すぐに信頼できるようにならなければ、彼らはその後もその人を信頼することはない。

（**C**）多様さと変化は彼らを用心深くさせる。

解説 後半の質問What did it take, when you think about it, to get those chimps to trust you?（チンパンジーに信頼してもらうには、振り返ってみると、何が必要だったと思うか）に対して、グドール氏は「急ぎすぎないことが大切だった」と答え、I wore the same-colored clothes every day so there was nothing new.（私は毎日同じ色の服を着た、［チンパンジーから見て］新しいものが現れないように）と付け加えている。ここから、チンパンジーが変化を嫌う警戒心の強い動物だとわかる。正解は（**C**）。

---

5. 正解 A

According to Goodall, how do chimpanzees reassure each other?

（**A**）By making physical contact
（**B**）By sitting down and waiting
（**C**）By giving each other palm-oil nuts

設問訳 グドール氏によると、チンパンジーはどのようにしてお互いを安心させるか。

（**A**）スキンシップをとる
（**B**）座って、待つ
（**C**）アブラヤシの実を与え合う

解説 後半のグドール氏の発言に、he took the nut and dropped it but very gently squeezed my fingers. That's how chimpanzees reassure each other.とある。ここのheとは、チンパンジーのデービッドのこと。squeezed my fingers（私の指を握った）を言い換えた選択肢は「スキンシップをとる」の（**A**）しかない。

問題文 **The following is an interview with well-known primatologist Jane Goodall.**

Fareed Zakaria Almost 60 years ago, Jane Goodall began her work that changed how we all think about animals. She traveled to Tanzania and ended up living among the species which is the closest relative to us humans. I started by asking her how her amazing career began.

Jane Goodall Well, I was 10 years old when I met Tarzan of the Apes in a little book and fell in love with him, and he married the wrong Jane. And so, it was [at] 10 years old when I had a dream: I will grow up, go to Africa, live with wild animals and write books about them. And everybody laughed at me. But my mother, my amazing mother, said, "If you really want something, you're going to have to work extremely hard, take advantage of all opportunity, but don't give up." And I've taken that message to young people, particularly in deprived communities.

So, anyway, the opportunity came when I had a boring job in London. I was invited to Kenya. I was 23, and I met the famous Louis Leakey. And he's the one who gave me the opportunity to go and live not with any animal but the one most like us, the chimpanzee.

I'd watched animals all my life. And I knew there was no...was nobody out there doing anything. So what I knew was, "I've got to get the...the chimpanzees to trust me so that I can learn about them." But the big problem was there was only money for six months. And the chimps were very shy, and they took one look at this weird, white ape and ran away.

But through my binoculars, I was beginning to learn about aspects of their behavior. And one chimpanzee, darling David Greybeard—he's the one I saw using and making tools to fish for termites. And it was that that enabled Leakey to go to [the] National Geographic Society. Not only did they agree to continue to fund the research, but they sent out a filmmaker, Hugo van Lawick, who became my husband.

Zakaria What did it take, when you think about it, to get those chimps to trust you?

Goodall Well, I think the important thing for me was not to push too fast. I wore the same-colored clothes every day so there was nothing new. And patience, patience. When you study animals, you simply must have patience.

Zakaria Was there a moment, or was it just a slow, incremental e...extending of their...of their trust to you?

Goodall There was one moment for me that was a

very seminal moment. I was actually following David through the forest, and I thought I'd lost him. And I came through this tangle of vegetation, and he was sitting. He was looking back, and I...it looked as though he was waiting for me, so I sat down near him. And there was a ripe, red oil-palm nut, which chimps love, so I held it out to him on my palm. And he turned his face away, so I put my hand closer. And he turned, he looked directly in my eyes, he reached out, he took the nut and dropped it but very gently squeezed my fingers. That's how chimpanzees reassure each other.

So in that moment, we communicated with each other perfectly in a gestural communication system that must have predated human words. And I think that was the moment when I thought, "This...this is what I have to do; I...I just have to carry on.

訳　著名な霊長類学者ジェーン・グドール氏への インタビューです。

ファリード・ザカリア　60年ほど前、ジェーン・グドール氏は皆の動物への認識を改めさせることになった仕事を開始しました。彼女はタンザニアへ赴き、やがて、われわれ人間に最も近い種と共に暮らすようになったのです。私はまず、彼女の驚異的なキャリアがどのようにして始まったのかを聞きました。

ジェーン・グドール　その、10歳の頃、私はある小さな本で「類猿人ターザン」に出会い、彼に恋をしました。でも、彼は間違ったジェーンと結婚してしまった。それで、私は10歳のときに夢を抱きました。大人になったらアフリカに行き、野生動物と共に暮らし、彼らについて本を書くという夢です。皆に笑われました。でも、私の母、素晴らしい母は言いました、「もし本当に何かを求めるなら、並々ならぬ努力をし、あらゆるチャンスをモノにしなければならないよ。でも諦めてはだめ」と。そして、私はそのメッセージを若い人たち、とりわけ困窮した地域の若者たちに伝えてきました。

それはともかく、チャンスがやってきたのは、私がロンドンでつまらない仕事に就いていたときのことでした。ケニアに行かないかと誘われたのです。当時私は23歳で、かの有名なルイス・リーキー氏に（ケニアで）出会いました。そして彼こそが、私にチャンスを与えてくれたのです、ほかでもない私たちヒトに最も近い動物、チンパンジーと共に暮らすというチャンスをね。

私は、それまでずっと動物たちを観察してきました。そして、（この分野について）何か研究している人は世界に誰もいないとわかっていました。ですから、私にわかっていたのは、「チンパンジーについて学ぶためには、彼らにこちらを信頼してもらう必要がある」ということでした。ですが、6カ月分のお金しかないというのが何よりの問題でした。それにチンパンジーはとても警戒心が強く、彼らはこの「奇妙な白っぽいサル」（＝グドール氏）を一目見ただけで逃げていきました。

でも、私は双眼鏡を通して、彼らの行動のいくつかの側面について学び始めていました。そしてある1匹のチンパンジー、愛らしい「白ひげのデービッド」ですが、私は彼がシロアリをつかまえるのに道具を使ったり、作ったりするのを見たのです。この発見のおかげで、リーキー氏は「ナショナル・ジオグラフィック協会」に（続きの資金を申請しに）行くことができました。協会は、調査への資金提供を継続することに同意してくれただけでなく、映像作家を送り込んできました。それがヒューゴ・バン・ラービックで、後に私の夫となった人です。

ザカリア　チンパンジーに信頼してもらうには、振り返ってみると、何が必要だったと思いますか。

グドール　そうですね、思うに、私にとって大切だったのは急ぎすぎないということでした。私は毎日同じ色の服を着ました、（チンパンジーから見て）新しいものが現れないようにね。あとはとにかく忍耐力です。動物を研究するときは、とにかく忍耐が必要なのです。

ザカリア　きっかけとなるような瞬間があったのですか、それとも、チンパンジーたちはあなたをただゆっくり、徐々に信頼してくれるようになったのですか。

グドール　私にとって、決定的な瞬間がありました。実は、私は（白ひげの）デービッドを追って森を歩いていたのですが、彼を見失ったと思いました。絡み合う草木をくぐり抜けると、彼が座っていました。こちらを振り返ったので私は……まるで彼が私を待っていたかのようでしたので、私は彼のそばに腰を下ろしました。そこに、チンパンジーの大好物の熟した赤いアブラヤシの実があったので、私はそれを手のひらに載せて彼に差し出しました。すると彼が顔を背けたので、私はもっと手を近づけました。そうすると彼はこちらを向き、まっすぐに私の目を見てから、手を差し出して、実を手に取って落としましたが、とても優しく私の指を握りました。それはチンパンジー同

士がお互いを安心させる方法なのです。

　ですからその瞬間、私たちは互いに、ヒトの言語よりも前に存在していたに違いない身ぶりによるコミュニケーション・システムによって、完璧に意思の疎通ができたのです。それがこう思った瞬間だったと思います、「これが私のやるべきことだ、これをやり続けるべきなんだ」って。

語句

primatologist: 霊長類学者／species: 種／relative: 同じ分類単位に属する動物／Tarzan of the Apes: 類猿人ターザン　▶「ターザン」は米作家のエドガー・ライス・バローズが創作したキャラクターおよび彼を主人公にした小説。／he married the wrong Jane: ▶「ターザン」の結婚相手の名前は「ジェーン」。グドール氏のファーストネームも「ジェーン」であることから、「ターザンは私と結婚すべきだった」という意味のジョーク。／deprived: 恵まれない、貧しい／Louis Leakey: ルイス・リーキー▶ケニアの著名な考古学者・人類学者。／chimp: ＝chimpanzee／shy: 〈動物が〉警戒心が強い／weird: 奇妙な、変な／binoculars: 双眼鏡／David Greybeard: ▶ grey beard は「グレーのあごひげ」の意味。／fish for: 〜を探す、探り出す／termite: シロアリ／patience: 忍耐／incremental: 〈変化などが〉徐々に起こる、ゆっくりとした／extend: （相手に対して感謝・同情・信頼などを）示す／seminal: （将来を変えるような）重大な、画期的な／tangle: （木の枝などの）もつれ／vegetation: 植物、草木／ripe: 熟した／oil palm: アブラヤシ／hold A out to B: AをBに差し出す／palm: 手のひら／squeeze: 〜を握る、つかむ／reassure: 〜を安心させる／predate: 〜より前から存在する／carry on: （仕事などを）続ける

No.2
問題文 46 設問 47
アメリカ英語 (Fareed Zakaria) ／アメリカ英語 (Chris Hughes)

1. 正解 B

What is the interview mainly about?
(A) Privacy in social media
(B) Concerns about Facebook
(C) The history of antitrust laws

設問訳 これは主に何についてのインタビューか。
(A) ソーシャルメディアにおけるプライバシー
(B) フェイスブックに対する懸念

(C) 独占禁止法の歴史

解説 インタビューの主旨をつかむには、インタビュアーがゲストを紹介する導入部分がヒントになる。My next guest says that Facebook is too big...in a *New York Times* opinion piece entitled "It's Time to Break Up Facebook." を要約すると、「今日のゲストはフェイスブックの共同創業者で、ニューヨーク・タイムズ紙に掲載された『フェイスブックを分割すべき時が来た』と題する意見記事を書いたクリス・ヒューズ氏である」となり、この後展開していくインタビューの内容が予想できる。よって、正解は (B)。(A) と (C) にも少し触れられてはいるが、インタビュー全体の主題ではない。

2. 正解 C

What view did the interviewer present about Facebook and the free market?
(A) Because Facebook is free, it has no responsibility to users.
(B) Facebook should pay users for the data they provide.
(C) Users agree to give up their privacy when they use Facebook.

設問訳 インタビュアーが示したフェイスブックと自由市場についての見解はどのようなものか。
(A) フェイスブックは無料なので、利用者に対する責任がない。
(B) フェイスブックは、利用者が提供するデータに対して利用者に金を支払うべきだ。
(C) 利用者はプライバシーを放棄することに同意した上でフェイスブックを使っている。

解説 ザカリア氏が「フェイスブックと自由市場」について述べているのは、when people choose to use Facebook... That's the free market.（利用者がフェイスブックを利用することを選ぶとき……それが自由市場というものだ）という箇所である。それを agree to do（〜することに同意する）＋ give up their privacy（プライバシーを放棄する）で簡潔に言い表したのが (C) である。

3. 正解 C

What did Hughes mean when he said that Facebook is not really free?
(A) Facebook cannot be considered a free service because it is a monopoly.

(**B**) It costs a lot of money to run a company like Facebook.

(**C**) Users give Facebook their data in exchange for using the service.

設問訳 ヒューズ氏は「フェイスブックは無料とは言えない」と、どのような意味で言ったのか。

(**A**) フェイスブックは独占企業なので、無料サービスとみなすことはできない。

(**B**) フェイスブックのような会社を運営するには多額の金がかかる。

(**C**) 利用者はサービスを利用する代わりに、フェイスブックにデータを提供している。

解説 ヒューズ氏が指摘する、フェイスブックが独占状態となっていることの問題点は、「いかなる競争もないから、説明責任を果たす義務もないこと」(without any kind of competition, there is no accountability) なので、(**A**) はおかしい。また、「莫大な運営費がかかっているので無料とは言えない」という話は出てこないので、(**B**) も不正解。ヒューズ氏の They don't pay with dollars, but they pay with their data and with their attention. (金銭ではなく、自分のデータと関心で支払っている) というコメントから、「利用者が提供している自分のデータと関心というものは、金銭を支払っているのも同然だ」という主張を読み取れるので、正解は (**C**)。

4. 正解 A

What is the accountability problem that Hughes mentioned?

(**A**) Mark Zuckerberg does not really have to answer to anyone.

(**B**) Facebook's board of directors has too much power over Zuckerberg.

(**C**) Facebook is subject to regulation by the FTC.

設問訳 ヒューズ氏が述べた説明責任に関係する問題とは何か。

(**A**) マーク・ザッカーバーグ氏はほとんど誰にも説明する義務がない。

(**B**) フェイスブックの取締役会はザッカーバーグ氏に対して力を持ちすぎている。

(**C**) フェイスブックは連邦取引委員会の規制対象となっている。

語句 be subject to: (規則などの) 影響下にある

解説 ヒューズ氏が問題視しているのは、「フェイスブックに説明責任がない」ことである。さらに、CEO であるマーク・ザッカーバーグ氏について、there is a board, but he...because he owns 60 percent of the voting shares, he's not accountable, really, to that board... He's not really accountable to users, and thus far, he's not been accountable to government. (取締役会はあるが、彼が議決権株式の60%を保有しているため、実際には、彼は取締役会に対して説明責任を負っていない……彼は事実、利用者に対しても説明責任を持たず、今のところ政府に対してもその責任を持たない) と述べている。これを言い換えた (**A**) が正解。

5. 正解 B

What did Hughes say about corporate governance?

(**A**) Making a profit should be the only goal of corporate governance.

(**B**) Corporations should fulfill a broad range of social responsibilities.

(**C**) Corporate boards do not have environmental responsibilities.

設問訳 ヒューズ氏は企業統治について何と述べたか。

(**A**) 利益を生み出すことが企業統治の唯一の目標であるべきだ。

(**B**) 企業は広範囲にわたる社会的責任を果たすべきだ。

(**C**) 取締役会は環境に対して責任を持たない。

解説 インタビューの後半で、ヒューズ氏は corporate governance (企業統治) について自身の考えを述べている。one thing...I think is really important is that we can approach corporate governance differently. (私が本当に大切だと考えているのは、企業統治に対して別の方法で働きかけることができるということ) と述べ、さらに boards have a responsibility not just to the bottom line but to customers, to suppliers, to the environment... (最終損益に対してだけでなく、顧客やサプライヤー、地球環境に対しても取締役会が責任を持つようにすべきだ) と述べている。よって、正解は (**B**)。

問題文 **The following is an interview with Chris Hughes, cofounder of Facebook.**

Fareed Zakaria My next guest says that Facebook is too big, Mark Zuckerberg is too powerful, the company needs to be split up. You probably would not expect such ideas from the cofounder of Facebook, Chris Hughes. But that is what Hughes put forth in a *New York Times* opinion piece entitled "It's Time to Break Up Facebook." And Chris Hughes, who was Zuckerberg's roommate at Harvard, joins me now.

The biggest argument against your position is that Facebook provides services for free to people, and when people choose to use Facebook, WhatsApp, Instagram, they are voluntarily ceding that privacy. They know that Facebook is using it. What's wrong with that? That's the free market.

Chris Hughes Well, I don't think that's quite right, for two reasons. First off, I think that users do pay quite a bit to use Facebook. They don't pay with dollars, but they pay with their data and with their attention. We are providing immense amounts of data. I think it's also not true because the space is so locked down, Facebook has become such a strong monopoly, that there's no alternative. So without any kind of competition, there's no accountability.

The long history of antitrust is that it's a way of holding businesses that have gotten too big and too powerful accountable. So it's built on the same principle of checks and balances that our founders outlined in the Constitution for the different branches of government, but for the private sector as well.

Zakaria Your biggest concern, you say in the piece, is the degree to which Mark Zuckerberg has almost total control over what information we all read about, access.

Hughes Yeah. You know, the way that Facebook is structured as a company... Mark's the CEO, there is a board, but he...because he owns 60 percent of the voting shares, he's not accountable, really, to that board. It works more like a board of advisers than anything else. He's not really accountable to users, and thus far, he's not been accountable to government.

So, one thing I don't spend time on in the piece but I think is really important is that we can approach corporate governance differently. There's a...a...a lot of folks who call for thinking about making sure that boards have a responsibility not just to the bottom line but to customers, to suppliers, to the environment, a kind of global responsibility, which, again, was what it was like in the '50s and '60s before the revolution over the past few years.

So I think that kind of thinking when applied to Facebook would immediately bring accountability to...to the company. Or if the FTC broke up the company, or if there were meaningful privacy regulation, that too would bring accountability. But the world that we're in right now is one where I do think Mark Zuckerberg has too much power, n...near unilateral power.

Zakaria Chris Hughes, pleasure to have you on.

Hughes Thanks for having me.

訳 **フェイスブックの共同創業者、
クリス・ヒューズ氏へのインタビューです。**

ファリード・ザカリア 次にお招きするゲストはこう言います、フェイスブックは大きすぎる、マーク・ザッカーバーグは権力を持ちすぎている、会社は分割されるべきだと。そのような考えがフェイスブックの共同創業者のクリス・ヒューズ氏から出てくるとは予想外のことでしょう。しかし、これはヒューズ氏がニューヨーク・タイムズ紙に掲載された「フェイスブックを分割すべき時が来た」と題する意見記事で提言したものです。ハーバードでザッカーバーグ氏のルームメートだったクリス・ヒューズ氏に今から加わっていただきます。

あなたの見解に対する最大の反論は、フェイスブックは人々にサービスを無料で提供しているし、利用者はフェイスブックやワッツアップ、インスタグラムを利用することを選ぶとき、自ら進んでプライバシーを譲渡している、というものです。フェイスブックがそのデータを利用することを彼らは知っている。それの何が問題なのか。それが自由市場というものだ、と。

クリス・ヒューズ その、私は2つの理由からそれは正しいとは言えないと考えています。まず、利用者はフェイスブックを利用するのに相当の対価を払っていると思います。金銭ではなく、自分のデータと関心で支払っている

のです。私たち利用者が（フェイスブックに）提供している情報量は膨大なものです。正しくないと考えるもう1つの理由は、その活動領域があまりに閉鎖的で、フェイスブックはあまりにも強大な独占企業となっているので、それに取って代わるものがないということです。そのため、いかなる競争もないから、説明責任を果たす義務もありません。

長い歴史を持つ反トラスト法は、あまりにも巨大で権力を持ちすぎた企業に説明責任を負わせる1つの方法です。つまり、それは、アメリカの建国の父たちが（権力を分散させるために）複数の政府機関に対して合衆国憲法に記したのと同じ抑制と均衡の原則に基づくものですが、民間部門にも当てはまります。

ザカリア あなたが記事に記していた最大の懸念は、私たちが読んだりアクセスしたりする情報を、マーク・ザッカーバーグ氏がほぼ完全に掌握しているという、その度合いですよね。

ヒューズ そうです。フェイスブックの会社としての形態は……マークがCEOで、取締役会はありますが、彼が議決権株式の60%を保有しているため、実際には、彼は取締役会に対して説明責任を負っていません。その役割はむしろ顧問委員会も同然です。彼は事実、利用者に対しても説明責任を持たず、今のところ政府に対してもその責任を持ちません。

記事ではあまり触れていませんが、私が本当に大切だと考えているのは、企業統治に対して別の方法ではたらきかけることができるということです。必ず取締役会に責任を持たせるようにするという考えを求める人は多いです、最終損益に対してだけでなく、顧客やサプライヤー、そして地球環境に対してもね。それは一種、世界規模の責任と言えるもので、この何（十）年かの間に起こった大きな変革の前の、50年代と60年代にはそうなっていたのです。

そのため私が思うに、その種の考え方がフェイスブックに適用されれば、ただちに同社に説明責任を負わせることになるでしょう。または連邦取引委員会が同社を分割させるか、効果的なプライバシー保護規制がもしあれば、それも（同社に）説明責任を負わせるでしょう。しかし、私たちが今いるこの世界は、思うに、マーク・ザッカーバーグがあまりにも大きな権力、ほとんど一方的な権力を持っている世界なのです。

ザカリア クリス・ヒューズさん、ご出演に感謝します。

ヒューズ こちらこそありがとう。

語句

cofounder: 共同設立者、共同創業者／powerful: 大きな力のある、影響力のある／split up: ～を分割する／put forth: （考えなどを）提唱する、発表する／opinion piece: 意見記事／entitle A B: AをBと題する／break up: （会社などを）分割する／argument against: ～に対する反論／position: 見解、見方／WhatsApp: ワッツアップ ▶スマホ向けチャットアプリ。／voluntarily: 自ら進んで／cede: （権利などを）譲渡する／free market: 自由市場／first off: まず、第一に／attention: 注意を向けること、関心を払うこと／immense: 多大な、膨大な／the space is locked down: その場所が封鎖されている ▶ここでは「活動領域が閉鎖的である」ということ。／monopoly: 独占企業／alternative: 代替物、代わりとなるもの／competition: 競争／accountability: 説明責任、説明の義務／antitrust: 独占禁止の、反トラストの ▶ここでは名詞としてantitrust lawやantitrust policyなどの意味で用いられている。／hold...accountable: …に責任を課す、責任を取らせる／business: 企業、会社／principle: 原則／checks and balances: 抑制と均衡 ▶国の立法、行政、司法の三権分立について言うことが多い。／founder: 建国者／outline: ～の概要を説明する、～の要点を述べる／the Constitution (of the United States): 合衆国憲法／branch of government: 政府機関 ▶立法、行政、司法の各機関。／private sector: 民間部門／degree: 度合い、程度／have total control over: ～を完全に支配する／structure: ～を構成する、組織する／board: 取締役会、役員会／voting share: 議決権株式／board of advisers: 顧問委員会／thus far: 今までのところは／corporate governance: 企業統治／folks: 人々／call for: ～を求める、呼びかける／make sure that: 確実に～であるようにする／have a responsibility to: ～に対して責任を持つ／the bottom line: 最終損益／supplier: 供給者、サプライヤー／apply A to B: AをBに適用する／FTC: ＝US Federal Trade Commission 米連邦取引委員会 ▶日本の公正取引委員会に相当。／meaningful: 意味のある／privacy regulation: プライバシー保護規制／near: ほぼ、ほとんど／unilateral: 一方的な、独断的な

Reading Section リーディング編

Part 1 語彙問題

No.1

正解 A

The wind turbine was designed specifically to **generate** power, and today, almost 4 percent of the world's electricity is produced by wind.

(**A**) generate　(**B**) project　(**C**) regulate

訳

風力タービンは特に発電を目的として設計され、今では世界の電力の4%近くが風力によって生み出されています。

語句

design: ～を設計する／ specifically: 特に、特別に／ generate power: 発電する／ project: ～を噴出する、放出する／ regulate: ～を規制する、統制する

No.2

正解 B

In 2016, the Chinese government changed the **notorious** one-child policy. Each couple is now allowed to have two babies.

(**A**) expensive　(**B**) notorious　(**C**) predictable

訳

2016年に、中国政府は悪名高き「一人っ子政策」を転換しました。現在、夫婦一組につき2人の赤ん坊を産むことが許されています。

語句

notorious:（悪いことで）有名な、悪名高い／ allow...to do: …が～することを許す／ predictable: 予測できる、ありきたりな

No.3

正解 A

Huge numbers of Cambodian migrants are fleeing Thailand. They are worried about a possible crackdown on **undocumented** workers.

(**A**) undocumented　(**B**) discredited
(**C**) unrecognizable

訳

おびただしい数のカンボジア人移民がタイから脱出しています。彼らは、不法就労者の取り締まりがあるかもしれないと懸念しています。

語句

migrant 移住者、移民／ flee: ～から逃げる／ crackdown on: ～に対する取り締まり／ undocumented worker: 不法就労者／ discredited: 信用を失った／ unrecognizable: 認識できない

No.4

正解 C

The Trump administration hopes to make military **inroads** into the final frontier, the depths of outer space.

(**A**) objections　(**B**) interventions　(**C**) inroads

訳

トランプ政権は最後の未開拓地、つまり、宇宙の深奥に軍事的進出を図りたいと考えています。

語句

administration: 政権／ make inroads into: ～に参入する、進出する／ military: 軍事的な／ frontier: 未開拓地、フロンティア／ depths: 奥まった所、深奥／ outer space: 宇宙／ objection: 反対、異議／ intervention: 介入

Part 2 短文読解問題

No.1

1. 正解 B

What is the news report mainly about?

(**A**) Lifestyle diseases

(**B**) Drug-resistant infections

(**C**) Drug overdoses

設問訳 このニュースは主に何について述べているか。

(**A**) 生活習慣病

(**B**) 薬剤耐性感染症

(**C**) 薬物の過剰摂取

解説 第1段落最後の Superbugs that cause drug-resistant forms of diseases are growing fast（薬剤耐性疾患を引き起こすスーパー耐性菌が急増している）の箇所から、ニュースのトピックは「薬剤耐性感染症」であるとわかる。よって、正解は（**B**）。

2. 正解 A

What kind of economic impact is expected?

(**A**) Costs will be very high around the world.

(**B**) The annual world GDP will increase.

(**C**) No impact is expected in Africa and Asia.

設問訳 どのような経済的影響が予測されるか。

(**A**) 世界中で損失額が非常に高くなる。

(**B**) 世界の年間GDPが増える。

(**C**) アフリカやアジアでの影響は予測されていない。

解説 第2段落の The study also talks about economic impact. に続く部分を読むと、It predicts that related global costs will spiral upwards to $100 trillion or more（その研究報告書は、関連する世界全体の損失は100兆ドル以上に急上昇すると予測している）とある。よって、正解は（**A**）。

問題文 The Growing Threat of Superbugs

According to a new report, drug-resistant infections are expected to dramatically increase across the globe. The main culprit is the overuse of antibiotics, which are not the solution we tend to think they are. Superbugs that cause drug-resistant forms of diseases are growing fast and may claim more lives than cancer by the year 2050.

The study also talks about economic impact. It predicts that related global costs will spiral upwards to $100 trillion or more, a figure larger than the current annual world GDP of $70 trillion.

The world's poorest nations are most at risk. Nine million of the estimated 10 million deaths will be in Africa and Asia. The aim of the study is to sound the alarm and call for global action.

訳 増大するスーパー耐性菌の脅威

新しい研究報告によると、世界中で薬剤耐性感染症の劇的な増加が見込まれているそうです。その主な原因は、抗生物質の過剰使用です。われわれは抗生物質を病気を完全に解決してくれるものと考えがちですが、そうではないのです。薬剤耐性疾患を引き起こすスーパー耐性菌が急増しており、2050年までにがんよりも多くの人の命を奪うかもしれません。

さらに、研究報告書はその経済的影響についても論じており、関連する世界全体の損失は100兆ドル以上に急上昇すると予測しています。その数字は現在の世界の年間GDP 70兆ドルよりも多いのです。

最もリスクが高いのは、世界の最貧諸国です。推計1000万人とされる死亡者のうち900万人がアフリカとアジアに集中することになるでしょう。この研究の目的は、警鐘を鳴らして世界規模の行動を求めることにあります。

語句

superbug: 薬剤耐性の強い細菌、スーパー耐性菌／drug-resistant: 薬剤耐性の／infection: 感染症／culprit:（問題の）原因／overuse: 過剰使用／antibiotics: 抗生物質／solution: 解決策／tend to do: 〜する傾向にある／disease: 病気、疾患／claim the life of: 〜の命を奪う／impact: 影響／predict that: 〜だと予測する／related: 関連のある／cost: 損失／spiral upwards to: 〜に急上昇する／trillion: 1兆／figure: 数字／annual: 年次の／estimated: 推計の、見積もりの／aim: 目的／sound the alarm: 警鐘を鳴らす／call for: 〜を呼び求める

No.2

---

1. 正解 A

What is the news report mainly about?

(A) Efforts to end slavery in the cocoa industry

(B) A new marketing approach for chocolate

(C) Ways to send ethical messages to consumers

設問訳 このニュースは主に何について述べているか。

(A) カカオ産業における奴隷制を終わらせる努力

(B) チョコレートの新しいマーケティング法

(C) 消費者に倫理的なメッセージを送る方法

解説 第1段落の冒頭文で「あるオランダの会社が奴隷制度をなくすために闘う（fight slavery）ことを決意している」とあり、さらに「カカオ産業では人身売買（trafficking）や児童労働（child labor）といった違法な労働慣習のもとで働く人々がいる」こと、つまり「（現代の）奴隷制度」について述べている。ここからニュースのテーマが読み取れるので、正解は（**A**）。

---

2. 正解 C

According to the 2015 study, why do the unethical practices continue?

(A) Because of trafficking

(B) Because of hazardous conditions

(C) Because of poverty

設問訳 2015年の調査によると、非倫理的な慣習が続いているのはなぜか。

(A) 人身売買のため

(B) 危険な状況のため

(C) 貧困のため

解説 第3段落で2015年の調査について言及されており、Endemic poverty was cited as a major reason why trafficking and unethical practices continue.「（この調査では）人身売買や非倫理的な慣習が今も続いている主な理由として、現地ではびこる貧困（poverty）が挙げられている」とある。よって、正解は（**C**）。

問題文　Chocolate for a Better World

A Dutch company is determined to fight slavery, and their weapon of choice is chocolate. More than 2 million people work in the cocoa industry under such illegal practices as trafficking and child labor, and Tony's Chocolonely wants to help fix that.

Tony's buys cocoa beans only from ethical farm cooperatives in West Africa. The beans are ground into liquid chocolate, which is then molded by Belgian chocolate masters. Each chocolate bar is stamped with unequal shapes to reflect inequality in the world, a reminder to chocolate consumers of why Tony's Chocolonely began.

However, labor abuses in cocoa production remain in the headlines. According to a 2015 study, more than 2 million child laborers are exposed to hazardous conditions. Endemic poverty was cited as a major reason why trafficking and unethical practices continue. Tony's believes their business model can improve the situation. They want to set an example for bigger companies toward solving the problem of slavery in the value chain of cocoa.

訳　より良い世界にするためのチョコレート

あるオランダの会社が（現代の）奴隷制度をなくすために闘うことを決意しています。そして彼らが武器に選んだのは、チョコレートです。カカオ産業では、200万人以上の人々が人身売買や児童労働といった違法な労働慣習のもとで働いており、トニーズ・チョコロンリー社はこの状況を改善するのに役立ちたいと考えています。

トニーズ社は西アフリカにある倫理的な農園協同組合からのみカカオ豆を仕入れます。その豆をひいて液体チョコレートを作ります。その後、ベルギーの熟練のチョコレート職人がそれを形成します。チョコレートバーの一本一本には、世界の不平等を反映するふぞろいな形の刻印が押されます。これはチョコレートの消費者になぜトニーズ・チョコロンリー社が生まれたのかを思い起こさせます。

しかし、カカオ生産における強制労働のニュースは今も報道されています。ある2015年の調査によると、（カカオ生産の現場で）200万人以上の児童労働者が危険な状況にさらされているということです。（この調査では）人身売買や非倫理的な慣習が今も続いている主な理由として、現地ではびこる貧困が挙げられています。トニー社は、自分たちのビジネスモデルは状況を改善することができると信じています。彼らは、カカオ産業の価値連鎖における奴隷制度問題の解決に向けて大企業に手本を示したいと考えています。

語句

Dutch: オランダの／be determined to do: 〜することを決意している／slavery: 奴隷制度／weapon of choice: 好んで使われる武器／cocoa: カカオ／illegal: 不法な、違法な／practice: 慣習、慣行／trafficking: 違法売買、違法取引／child labor: 児童労働／fix: (問題などを)解決する／ethical: 倫理的な、道徳上の／farm cooperative: 農場協同組合／grind A into B: AをすりつぶしてBにする／mold: 〜を成形する／stamp: 〜に(模様・記号などを)刻印する／unequal: ふぞろいな、等しくない／reflect: 〜を表す、反映する／inequality: 不平等／reminder: 思い起こさせるもの・人／consumer: 消費者／labor abuse: 強制労働／(be) in the headlines: ニュースになっている、報道されている／child laborer: 児童労働者／be exposed to: (雨風や危険などに)さらされている／hazardous: 危険な、有害な／endemic: (ある地域や集団に)特有の、よく見られる／poverty: 貧困、貧乏／cite A as B: AをBとして引き合いに出す／unethical: 非倫理的な／set an example for: 〜に手本を示す／value chain: 価値連鎖、バリューチェーン ➤購買から製造、営業などの各プロセスで改善や連携を考えること。

No.3

1. 正解 A

What is the main point of the news report?

(A) A new smell sensor has been developed.

(B) A new device is being used to detect diseases in dogs.

(C) Technology is helping people who have lost their sense of smell.

設問訳 このニュースの主旨は何か。

(A) 新しい嗅覚センサーが開発された。

(B) 新しい装置が犬の病気を検知するのに使われている。

(C) 技術が嗅覚を失った人々の役に立っている。

解説 第1段落の2文目で、an extraordinary sensor is now helping humans to sniff the air for anything dangerous, including diseases（驚くべきセンサーのおかげで人間も、空気中から危険なものを嗅ぎ分けやすくなりつつある、病気も含めて）とあるので、(A) が正解と判断できる。なお、このセンサーは「病気を検知する」と

2. 正解 B

Where will the new device be used after it is made even smaller?

(A) In the pet industry

(B) In the healthcare market

(C) In fingerprinting

設問訳 この新しい装置はさらに小型化されたらどこで利用されるか。

(A) ペット業界で

(B) 医療分野の市場で

(C) 指紋採取で

解説 第4段落の2文目で、It is already tiny, but work continues to shrink it further for the healthcare market.（現状でも小さなものだが、医療分野の市場に向けてさらに小型化すべく、取り組みが続けられている）とある。よって、(B) が正解。

問題文　Sniffing Out Danger

Dogs have a sense of smell that is infinitely better than ours. However, an extraordinary sensor is now helping humans to sniff the air for anything dangerous, including diseases.

The sensor is a microchip that detects chemicals in the air, and it works like a tiny digital nose. It uses the unique fingerprint of a chemical to identify it among all the molecules present in the air.

The sensor can be used in different ways. It can detect different sorts of smells and can also tell how much of something is present. It can detect down to levels of parts per billion. That's equivalent to one drop in an Olympic-size swimming pool.

The microchip was developed by combining expertise in chemistry, electronics and nanotechnology. It is already tiny, but work continues to shrink it further for the healthcare market. The plan is to use the microchip in mobile phones to detect compounds on the breath that indicate illnesses like cancer, tuberculosis and asthma.

訳　危険を嗅ぎ取る

犬の嗅覚はわれわれ人間とは比べものにならないほど

優れています。しかし、驚くべきセンサーのおかげで人間も、空気中から危険なものを嗅ぎ分けやすくなりつつあります、病気も含めて。

そのセンサーは空気中の化学物質を検知するマイクロチップで、ごく小さなデジタル式の鼻のような役目をします。それはある化学物質に特有の特徴をたよりに、空気中にあるすべての分子の中から、その化学物質を識別します。

そのセンサーはさまざまな使い方ができます。それは異なる種類のにおいを検知し、さらに、そのものがどのくらいあるかもわかります。10億分の1のレベルまで検出が可能です。それはオリンピックサイズのプールに垂らした1滴にほぼ等しい量です。

このマイクロチップは科学、電子工学、ナノテクノロジーの技術を結集して開発されました。センサーは現状でも小さなものですが、医療分野の市場に向けてさらに小型化すべく、取り組みが続けられています。このマイクロチップを携帯電話に組み込んで、呼気に含まれる化合物を検知し、がんや結核、ぜんそくなどの病気を発見

できるようにする計画です。

語句

sniff out: 〜を嗅ぎ分ける／a sense of smell: 嗅覚／infinitely:《比較級の前で》はるかに、比べものにならないほど／extraordinary: 驚くべき、並外れた／sniff A for B: AからBを嗅ぎ分ける／detect: 〜を検知する、検出する／chemical: 化学物質／fingerprint: 顕著な特徴／identify: 〜を特定する、識別する／molecule: 分子／(be) present: (そこに)ある、存在する／parts per billion: 10億分の1／be equivalent to: 〜と同等である、等しい／combine: 〜をまとめる、統合する／expertise in: 〜の専門的技術、専門的知識／shrink: 〜を縮小する、小さくする／compound: 化合物／indicate: 〜のしるしである、〜を示す／cancer: がん／tuberculosis: 結核／asthma: ぜんそく

Part 3 長文読解問題

No.1

1. 正解 A

What is the main topic of the news report?
(**A**) The purpose of Nigeria's space program
(**B**) Efforts to improve Nigeria's electricity supply
(**C**) Nigeria's plan to put the first African astronaut on the moon

設問訳 このニュースの主題は何か。
(**A**) ナイジェリアの宇宙計画の目的
(**B**) ナイジェリアの電力供給を改善する努力
(**C**) 初のアフリカ人宇宙飛行士を月へ送るというナイジェリアの計画

解説 第2段落のNASRDA局長の言葉に注目。「ナイジェリアの宇宙計画は当初からずっと、ナイジェリアが抱える問題に現実的な解決策を見いだすことを重視してきた」とあり、(**A**) がニュースの主題であるとわかる。(**B**) の「電力供給を改善すること」はナイジェリアが解決すべき問題の1つにすぎず、ニュース全体の主題とは言えない。

2. 正解 B

What does the news report say about Nigeria's space program?
(**A**) It boosts the country's economy by creating new jobs.
(**B**) It is not well known.
(**C**) Its laboratories have cutting-edge technology.

設問訳 このニュースはナイジェリアの宇宙計画について何と報じているか。
(**A**) 新しい仕事を創出することで、国の経済を後押ししている。
(**B**) あまり知られていない。
(**C**) その実験室には最先端テクノロジーがある。

語句 boost: 〜を後押しする／cutting-edge: 最先端の

解説 第3段落のIt might seem surprising that Nigeria...would fund a space program. Even Nigerians who work there have had a hard time believing it.や、when I tell my friends..."Oh, we have such an agency?"などの記述を読めば、正解は (**B**) だとわかる。

3. 正解 A

According to the news report, for what purpose has Nigeria used satellite images?

(A) To find solutions to some of the country's social problems

(B) To improve its electricity supply

(C) To look for habitable places on Mars

設問訳 このニュースによると、ナイジェリアは何のために衛星写真を使ったか。

(A) 国の一部の社会問題の解決策を見つけるため

(B) 電力供給を向上させるため

(C) 火星で居住可能な場所を見つけるため

語句 habitable: 居住可能な

解説 第4段落の researchers here say satellite images are...big problems like rapid urbanization, a swelling population and a looming food crisis から、正解は (A) となる。

4. 正解 B

What is a new goal that Nigeria hopes to achieve in the future?

(A) To open a museum to exhibit the country's achievements in space

(B) To build a satellite in Nigeria

(C) To use satellite images to understand shifts in population

設問訳 ナイジェリアが今後成し遂げたい新たな目標は何か。

(A) 同国の宇宙での功績を展示する博物館を開くこと

(B) ナイジェリアで人工衛星を製造すること

(C) 人口の変化を知るために衛星写真を使うこと

解説 第6段落に Handling such operations within Nigeria itself is the next goal. とあり、これが新たな目標である。第5段落最後の those satellites were not built or launched on Nigerian soil という記述、それに続く第6段落冒頭の So far, Nigeria's space program has outsourced its heavy lifting. から、such operations は「ナイジェリア国内で衛星を製造し、打ち上げること」だとわかる。よって、正解は (B)。

5. 正解 A

What does Mohammed probably think about NASA?

(A) Its achievements are worth the money spent on it.

(B) Too much money has been wasted on it.

(C) It should focus more on agriculture and the environment.

設問訳 モハメド氏は NASA について、おそらくどのように考えていると思われるか。

(A) NASA の業績はつぎ込んだ金額だけの価値がある。

(B) NASA にはあまりにも多くの資金が無駄につぎ込まれてきた。

(C) NASA はもっと農業や環境に焦点を当てるべきだ。

解説 最終段落の最後の部分でモハメド氏の考え方がわかる。Is money for the space agency a waste? To me, it is not. と疑問文に答える形で「宇宙開発への支出は無駄遣いではない」という考えを述べている。よって、正解は (A)。米国でよく出る質問の例として挙げた Why waste money on NASA? に惑わされないようにしよう。

問題文 Nigeria's Little-Known Space Program

When you think about space exploration, Cape Canaveral and the International Space Station probably come to mind. Here is another place to add to that list: Nigeria. That's right, Nigeria has a space program, implemented by the National Space Research and Development Agency (NASRDA).

"We're not part of the race for the moon. We're not part of the race for Mars. The space program in Nigeria has always been focused on bringing practical solutions to Nigeria's problems," says Seidu Onailo Mohammed, NASRDA's director general.

It might seem surprising that Nigeria, a country with spotty electricity, a 70 percent poverty rate and a life expectancy of 53 years, would fund a space program. Even Nigerians who work there have had a hard time believing it. Sadiya Bindir, an engineer at NASRDA says, "I was initially surprised that Nigeria had a space agency, and now when I tell my friends where I work, they're all, like, 'Oh, we have such an agency?'"

But researchers here say satellite images are key to understanding big problems like rapid urbanization, a swelling population and a looming food crisis. The space agency is also using its satellites to look for almost 300 schoolgirls kidnapped in 2014 by Boko Haram.

The agency has eight locations, including the Centre for Satellite Technology Development （CSTD） in the capital city, Abuja. Its sprawling campus is home to a ground station, a conference center and even a museum. The laboratories look more like high school science classrooms. But the agency has put five satellites in orbit since 2003. However, those satellites were not built or launched on Nigerian soil.

So far, Nigeria's space program has outsourced its heavy lifting. For example, Russia and China have launched Nigeria's previous Earth-observation and communication satellites. Handling such operations within Nigeria itself is the next goal. CSTD's Abubakar Sadiq Umar, an engineer who worked on those designs, says it is a matter of national pride: "We should be able to take what we've seen abroad and transplant it here in Nigeria so that we can have our own satellite that we'll be proud of."

Perhaps the most ambitious goal is to put the first African astronaut into space by 2030. "Putting a man in space," says Umar, "is one thing everybody tends to appreciate, and is a goal that every country wishes to actualize. And my country, Nigeria, cannot be left out."

Nigeria has allocated about $20 million to the space agency for the current year. But why should the government be spending so much money during these tough economic times? Director General Mohammed says more money is always needed: "This is the same question that has always been asked in the US. 'Why waste money on NASA?' But a budget for satellites is also a budget for agriculture, and it's also a budget for the environment. Is money for the space agency a waste? To me, it is not."

訳　ナイジェリアのあまり知られていない宇宙計画

宇宙開発と言えば、おそらくケープ・カナベラルや国際宇宙ステーションを思い浮かべるでしょう。そのリストに、新たな場所が加わります。ナイジェリアです。そう、ナイジェリアには宇宙計画があるのです。そして、それを実行するのは「国家宇宙研究開発機関」（NASRDA）です。

「われわれは、月面探査の競争に加わっているのではありません。火星探査の競争にも加わっていません。ナイジェリアの宇宙計画は当初からずっと、ナイジェリアが抱える問題に現実的な解決策を見いだすことを重視してきました」と、NASRDA局長のセイデュ・オナイロ・モハメド氏は言います。

意外だと思われるかもしれません、ナイジェリア、すなわち電力供給にむらがあり、貧困率70％、平均寿命53歳という国が、宇宙計画に資金を割いているなんて。この機関で働くナイジェリア人でさえ、にわかには信じられなかったと言います。NASRDAのエンジニアであるサディヤ・ビンディル氏は、「ナイジェリアに宇宙機関があることに最初は驚きました。私が友人に、どこで働いているかを話すと、みんなこう言うのです、『え、この国にそんな機関があるの？』って」と言います。

しかし、ここで働く研究者たちによれば、衛星写真が、急速な都市化、膨れ上がる人口、迫り来る食糧危機といった深刻な問題を理解するための重要な鍵になるということです。この宇宙機関は、2014年にボコ・ハラムによって誘拐された300人近くの女子生徒を捜すのにも人工衛星を利用しています。

この機関は8つの施設を持ち、その1つに、首都アブジャにある衛星技術開発センター（CSTD）があります。その広大な敷地には、地上局や会議場、博物館まであります。実験室は、どちらかというと高校の理科室のように見えます。しかし、この機関は2003年以来、5基の人工衛星を軌道に乗せてきました。それでも、それらの衛星はナイジェリア国内で製造し、打ち上げられたものではありません。

これまでナイジェリアの宇宙計画では、手間のかかる難事業を外部委託してきました。たとえば、ロシアや中国が、同国の以前の地球観測用または通信用の人工衛星を打ち上げてきたのです。ナイジェリア国内でそうした事業を行うことが次の目標です。それらの衛星の設計に携わったCSTDエンジニア、アブバカル・サディク・ウマール氏は、それは国の威信の問題だと言います。「外国で見てきたことを、ここナイジェリアで実現できるようにするべきです。そうすれば、誇るべき自前の人工衛星を持てるようになります」。

おそらく最も野心的な目標、それは2030年までに初のアフリカ人宇宙飛行士を宇宙に送ることです。「宇宙に人を送ることは」とウマール氏は言います、「だいたい誰もが評価することですし、どの国も実現を望んでいる目標です。わが国ナイジェリアも、そこから外れるわけにはいきません」。

ナイジェリアは今年、宇宙機関におよそ2000万ドルを充ててきました。しかし、この厳しい経済状況の中、なぜ政府はそれほどの額をつぎ込むべきなのでしょうか。モハメド局長によれば、さらなる資金が常に必要だということです。「これは、米国でもずっと問われてきた質問です。『なぜNASAに無駄な金をつぎ込むのか』と。しかし、人工衛星のための予算は、農業のための予算でもあり、環境のための予算でもあるのです。宇宙機関への支出は無駄遣いか？ 私に言わせれば、そんなことはありません」。

語句

space exploration: 宇宙開発／Cape Canaveral: ケープ・カナベラル ▶米国フロリダ半島東岸の岬。米航空宇宙局（NASA）のケネディ宇宙センターなどがある。／the International Space Station: ＝ISS 国際宇宙ステーション／come to mind: 心に浮かぶ、心をよぎる／add to: ～に加わる／implement: ～を実施する／Mars: 火星／practical: 現実的な、実際的な／director general: 長官、会長、局長／spotty: むらのある、よかったり悪かったりする／poverty rate: 貧困率／life expectancy: 平均寿命／fund: ～に資金を提供する／have a hard time doing: ～するのに苦労する、なかなか～できない／initially: 初めは、初めのうちは／satellite image: 衛星写真、衛星画像／urbanization: 都市化／swelling: 膨れ上がりつつある、増加する／looming: 迫りつつある、迫り来る／kidnap: ～を誘拐する／Boko Haram: ボコ・ハラム ▶ナイジェリア北部のイスラム過激派組織。／location: 施設、本部や支部／capital city: 首都／sprawling: 広々とした、だだっ広い／campus: 構内、敷地／be home to: (主語に)～がある／ground station: 地上局／conference center: 会議場／laboratory: 実験室、研究室／put...in orbit: …を軌道に乗せる／launch: ～を打ち上げる／soil: 国土、領土／outsource: (業務を)外部に委託する／heavy lifting: 困難で手間のかかる仕事／Earth-observation: 地球観測用の／communication satellite: 通信衛星／operation: 活動／a matter of: ～の問題／transplant: ～に移し替える／ambitious: 野心的な／astronaut: 宇宙飛行士／tend to do: ～する傾向にある、～しがちである／appreciate: ～を正当に評価する／actualize: ～を実現する／leave...out: …を考慮から外す／allocate: ～を割り当てる／current year: 今年／tough: 厳しい／budget: 予算／agriculture: 農業

No.2

---

1. 正解 A

What is the main problem that the report identifies?

(A) America has become deeply divided.

(B) Immigration issues are America's biggest concern.

(C) America is facing a slowing economy.

設問訳 この記事が指摘する主な問題点は何か。

(A) アメリカは深く分断している。

(B) 移民問題はアメリカ最大の懸念事項である。

(C) アメリカは不景気に直面している。

解説 第4段落の We see the forces that are pulling America apart. The question we should be focused on is, what can we do to bring the country together? から、著者の最も言いたいことは(A)であると判断できる。

---

2. 正解 A

What did Mark Muro conclude about the United States?

(A) That most of its recent economic growth has happened in cities

(B) That its small towns have been expanding rapidly

(C) That its urban areas and rural areas have been developing at an even pace

---

設問訳 マーク・ムーロ氏がアメリカについて結論づけたことは何か。

(A) 近年の経済成長のほとんどが都市で起きている

(B) 小規模町村が急速に拡大している

(C) 都会と地方は同じペースで発展している

語句 conclude that: ～ということを結論づける／even: 同等の

解説 第2段落で、the 53 largest American metro areas have accounted for...and a staggering three-quarters of all of its economic growth（規模において上位53カ所のアメリカ大都市圏が……そして驚くことに経済成長全体の4分の3もの割合を占めている）という説明に加えて、In fact, half of all job growth in the United States took place in just 20 cities.（実は全米における雇用拡大の半数はわずか20の都市で起こった）と述べられているので、「成長は都市部に偏ってい

る」と言える。そのため、（**C**）は誤りであり、（**A**）が正解。

---

3. 正解 C

What does the reporter mean by "two-track culture" in the third paragraph?
(**A**) Identity politics versus multiculturalism
(**B**) Immigrants versus Americans
(**C**) Rural culture versus urban culture

設問訳 第3段落で記者の言う「二層化した文化」とはどのような意味か。
(**A**) アイデンティティー・ポリティクスvs多文化主義
(**B**) 移民vsアメリカ国民
(**C**) 地方文化vs都市文化

解説 two-track culture（二層化した文化）の具体的な内容は、第3段落の with urbanites and rural Americans... They live different lives and disagree deeply about politics（都市住民と地方のアメリカ人が……互いに異なる生活を送り、政治について深く対立している）に示されている。正解は（**C**）。

---

4. 正解 B

Why is John F. Kennedy mentioned in the news report?
(**A**) Because Kennedy wrote a book on national service
(**B**) To illustrate the point about wealthy youth working for the national good
(**C**) Because Kennedy started a program like the one the reporter recommends

設問訳 このニュースでジョン・F・ケネディの名前が挙げられているのはなぜか。
(**A**) ケネディが国家奉仕についての本を書いたから
(**B**) 国家奉仕のために働く裕福な若者について例を挙げて説明するため
(**C**) 記者が推薦しているようなプログラムをケネディが始めたから

解説 第6段落で、ケネディはthe wealthy graduate of Choate and Harvard, famously served in World War II...（裕福でチョートとハーバードの出身だったが、よく知られているように、第二次世界大戦に従軍し……）と述べられており、このような経歴は、記者がthe sons and daughters of hedge-fund managers...working in public schools or national parks or the armed forcesと述

---

5. 正解 C

What does the reporter say about national service?
(**A**) It could take away many existing jobs.
(**B**) It is too much of a sacrifice for young Americans.
(**C**) It might be a way to bring Americans together again.

設問訳 記者は国家奉仕について何と言っているか。
(**A**) 今ある多くの仕事を奪う可能性がある。
(**B**) アメリカの若者にとって過度な犠牲的行為である。
(**C**) 再びアメリカを1つにする方法かもしれない。
語句 sacrifice: 犠牲的行為

解説 最終段落で、National service will not solve all of America's problems（国家奉仕がアメリカのあらゆる問題を解決するわけではない）と認めながらも、「既存の仕事が奪われる」「若者にとって犠牲的行為である」といった「国家奉仕」の具体的なデメリットについては触れていない。したがって（**A**）（**B**）は不適切。結論部にあるit might just help bring us together as a nation（私たちを1つの国家として団結させる助けにはなるかもしれない）という記述を言い換えた（**C**）が正解となる。

問題文 **National Service for National Unity**

The American economy is on solid footing. Now in its 120th month of expansion, it shows few signs of bubbles about to burst. Unemployment is way down, inflation is contained, and wages are finally moving up. And perhaps most significantly, productivity is up. There is no denying that economic indicators are firmly positive.

These good numbers, however, are unlikely to change another set of numbers, regarding the geography of growth. Mark Muro of the Brookings Institution has calculated that over the last decade, the 53 largest American metro areas have accounted for 71 percent of America's total population growth, two-thirds of all of its employment growth, and a staggering three-quarters of all of its economic growth. In fact, half of all job growth in the United States took place in just 20 cities. Meanwhile, small towns in rural America have lost residents and barely contributed anything to economic growth.

This two-track economy has produced a two-track culture, with urbanites and rural Americans increasingly living in their own distinct worlds of news, entertainment and consumer goods. They live different lives and disagree deeply about politics—a trend that is reflected in Washington.

Why is this happening? The economic trends can be explained by the digital revolution and globalization, in which brain work is more valuable, brawn work less so. The cultural forces are related to the recent rise of identity politics and backlash against immigration and multiculturalism. We see the forces that are pulling America apart. The question we should be focused on is, what can we do to bring the country together? Surely this has become the question of our times.

One answer that I have been increasingly drawn to is national service. There are many ways to design a national-service program, and a voluntary system will probably work better if it has strong incentives, like loan forgiveness and tuition support, at its core. A 2013 study argued that current programs could feasibly be scaled up to 1 million volunteers without taking jobs from existing workers and would yield societal benefits worth more than four times the cost of the programs. And the programs that are already in operation, such as AmeriCorps, do good work and have stunningly high approval ratings from their alumni. Ninety-four percent say they gained a better understanding of differing communities, and 80 percent say the program helped their careers.

As Mickey Kaus noted in a prescient 1992 book, John F. Kennedy, the wealthy graduate of Choate and Harvard, famously served in World War II on a PT boat alongside men who held jobs like mechanic, factory worker, truck driver and fisherman. Imagine if in today's America, the sons and daughters of hedge-fund managers, tech millionaires and bankers spent a year with the children of coal miners and farmers, working in public schools or national parks or the armed forces.

National service will not solve all of America's problems, but it might just help bring us together as a nation, and that is the crucial first step forward.

訳 国の結束のための国家奉仕

アメリカの経済は強固な基盤の上にあります。現在、その（景気）拡大は120カ月目に入っており、バブルがはじけそうな兆候はほとんど見られません。失業率はずっと下がっており、インフレは抑え込まれ、ついに賃金も上昇し始めています。そしておそらく最も注目すべきことに、生産性が向上しています。経済指標が確実に上向きであることは否定しようがありません。

しかし、こうした良い数字は経済成長の地理的分布に関する、別の一連の数値を変えそうにはありません。ブルッキングス研究所のマーク・ムーロ氏の算出によれば、過去10年を通じて、規模において上位53カ所のアメリカ大都市圏が、同国の人口増加全体の71%、雇用成長全体の3分の2、そして驚くことに経済成長全体の4分の3もの割合を占めています。実は（同期間に）全米における雇用拡大の半数はわずか20の都市で起こりました。一方、アメリカの地方の小規模町村は住民を失い、経済成長にほとんど何ら寄与していないのです。

この二層化した経済は、二層化した文化を生み出しており、都市住民と地方のアメリカ人が、以前にもましてそれぞれ独自のニュースやエンターテインメント、消費財から成る世界で暮らすようになっています。互いに異なる生活を送り、政治について深く対立している──これは米国政界にも反映されている傾向です。

なぜこうした事態が生じているのでしょうか。この経済動向はデジタル革命とグローバリゼーションによって説明できます。それらにおいては頭脳仕事により価値があり、力仕事にはそれほど価値が置かれないのです。文化的勢力は、近年のアイデンティティー・ポリティクスの台頭と、移民や多文化主義への反発と関連しています。アメリカを引き裂くそうした諸勢力は（十分）見えています。私たちが焦点を当てるべき問題、それは国を1つにまとめるために私たちにできることは何かということです。これはおそらく現代の最も重要な問題となっているでしょう。

私がますます引きつけられるようになっている解決策の1つは、国家奉仕です。国家奉仕プログラムを企画する方法は多数あり、自発的な奉仕で、ローン免除や授業料援助といった強力なインセンティブを中心に据えたシステムであればよりうまくいくでしょう。2013年のある研究によれば、現行のプログラムは、既存の就労者から職を奪うことなく、ボランティアを100万人にまで拡大する

ことが実現可能で、プログラムの経費の4倍以上に相当する社会的利益を生み出すだろうとのことです。そして、アメリコーをはじめとするすでに実施中のプログラムが優れた成果を上げており、その元参加者から驚くほど高い評価を獲得しています。94％が自分とは考えや生活を異にするコミュニティーへの理解が深まったとし、80％が自分のキャリアにとってプラスになったとしています。

ミッキー・カウス氏が1992年の予言的な著書で記したように、ジョン・F・ケネディは裕福でチョート（・ローズマリー・ホール）とハーバードの出身でしたが、よく知られているように、第二次世界大戦中、PTボート（哨戒魚雷艇）に配属され、機械工や工場労働者、トラック運転手、漁師といった職に就いていた人たちと共に兵役に服していました。もし今日のアメリカで、ヘッジファンド経営者やIT界のミリオネア、銀行家の息子たちや娘たちが、炭鉱作業員や農家の子どもたちと共に1年を過ごし、公立学校や国立公園、軍隊で活動するとしたらどうなるでしょう。

国家奉仕がアメリカのあらゆる問題を解決するわけではありませんが、私たちを1つの国家として団結させる助けにはなるかもしれません。そして、それは前進のために欠かせない初めの一歩なのです。

語句

national service: 国家奉仕／solid footing: 強固な基盤／expansion: 拡大／sign: 兆候、兆し／bubble: バブル景気／（be）about to do: まさに〜しようとしている／burst: 破裂する、はじける／unemployment: 失業率、失業者数／contain: 〜を抑える、抑制する／wage: 賃金、給料／significantly: 重要なことには／productivity: 生産性／there is no doing: 〜することはできない／deny that: 〜ということを否定する／economic indicator: 経済指標／firmly: 堅く、しっかりと／positive: 望ましい、プラスの／regarding: 〜に関して／geography: 地理、地勢／calculate that: 〜ということを算出する／metro area: 大都市圏／account for: 〜の割合を占める／population growth: 人口増加／staggering: 〈数量が〉驚くべき／take place: 起こる、生じる／rural: 田舎の、地方の／barely: ほとんど〜ない／contribute A to B: AをBに提供する、与える／two-track: 二重の／urbanite: 都市住民／increasingly: ますます／one's own distinct: 独自の／consumer goods: 消費財／trend: 傾向、動向／be reflected in: 〜に反映される／Washington: 米国政府／brain work: 頭脳仕事／brawn work: 力仕事／force: 勢力／be related to: 〜と関係がある／identity

politics: アイデンティティー・ポリティクス ▶特定のアイデンティティー（ジェンダー、人種、性的指向など）に基づく集団の利益を追求する政治活動のこと。／backlash against: 〜に対する反発／multiculturalism: 多文化主義／pull...apart: …を引き裂く／bring...together: …を団結させる／our times: 現代／be drawn to: 〜に引きつけられる／voluntary: 自発的な、志願制の／incentive: 刺激、誘引／forgiveness: 免除／tuition support: 学費支援／at its core: その中核に／current: 現行の、現在の／feasibly: 実行できるように／scale A up to B: AをBまで増やす／existing: 既存の／yield: 〜を産出する／societal benefit: 社会的利益／be in operation: 実施されている／AmeriCorps: アメリコー ▶米国の地域社会活動組織。公園清掃から災害援助まで、さまざまな奉仕活動を行う。／stunningly: 驚くほど／approval rating: 支持率／alumni: 卒業生たち ▶ alumna（女性）とalumnus（男性）の複数形。ここではプログラムの「元参加者たち」という意味。／Mickey Kaus: ミッキー・カウス ▶米国のジャーナリスト、評論家。／note（that）: 〜ということを指摘する／a prescient 1992 book: ▶ミッキー・カウスの著書 The End of Equality のこと。prescient は「予知の、予測の」の意味。／graduate: 卒業生／Choate: = Choate Rosemary Hall チョート・ローズマリー・ホール ▶米国の名門寄宿学校。／famously: よく知られているように／serve: 軍務に服する／PT boat: = patrol torpedo boat 哨戒魚雷艇／alongside: 〜と一緒に／hedge-fund manager: ヘッジファンド経営者／tech: テクノロジー企業の／banker: 銀行家、銀行経営者／coal miner: 炭鉱労働者／the armed forces: 軍隊／crucial: きわめて重大な、決定的な／step forward: 前進の一歩

読者アンケートにご協力ください。

お手数ですが、下記のURLまたはQRコードからアンケートへのご回答をお願いいたします。
ご意見を「CNN英語検定」の広告、弊社HPなどに転載させていただくことがあります。
ご了承ください。

アンケート回答URL（ブラウザの検索窓ではなく、URL入力窓に入力してください）

https://forms.gle/FpsspbqVbf8t6gWi8

笹尾洋介（ささお ようすけ）

京都大学 国際高等教育院附属国際学術言語教育センター 准教授。
京都大学総合人間学部卒業（2005年）、京都大学大学院人間・環境学研究科博士前期課程修了（2007年）。
ニュージーランド ヴィクトリア大学ウェリントン校（Victoria University of Wellington）より博士号を取得（2013年）。
応用言語学博士（Ph.D. in Applied Linguistics）。2012年より豊橋技術科学大学 総合教育院 講師を勤め、
准教授を経て、2017年より現職。外国語としての英語教育を専門とする。とくに、言語テスト、
語彙習得、教育文法、教材開発、学術目的の英語などに関する研究論文を多数発表している。

オンラインで受けられる
CNN英語検定公式ガイド

2020年7月5日　初版第1刷発行

監修	....	笹尾洋介（京都大学 国際高等教育院附属国際学術言語教育センター 准教授）
発行人	....	原 雅久
発行所	....	株式会社 朝日出版社
		〒101-0065
		東京都千代田区西神田 3 - 3 - 5
		TEL 03-3263-1230
		FAX 03-3239-7713
		https://www.asahipress.com/（HP）
		https://twitter.com/asahipress_com/（ツイッター）
		https://www.facebook.com/CNNEnglishExpress（フェイスブック）
印刷・製本	....	図書印刷株式会社
表紙デザイン・DTP	......	大串幸子
表紙画像	....	DenPhotos/Shutterstock.com、Prostock-studio/Shutterstock.com
音声録音・編集	....	ELEC（一般財団法人 英語教育協議会）

© Asahi Press, 2020 All Rights Reserved. Printed in Japan ISBN978-4-255-01189-9 C0082
TM & © 2020 Turner Broadcasting System, Inc. A WarnerMedia Company. All Rights Reserved.